The Ultimate Self-Teaching Method!

Play Banjo Today!

A Complete Guide to the Basics

PLAYBACK+
Speed • Pitch • Balance • Loop

To access audio and video visit:
www.halleonard.com/mylibrary
Enter Code
1477-3675-1544-6972

by Colin O'Brien

Recording Credits:
Colin O'Brien, Banjo, Guitar & Narration
Recorded at Buckaroo Studios,
Milwaukee, WI

ISBN 978-1-5400-5239-1

HAL•LEONARD®

Copyright © 2010, 2011 by HAL LEONARD CORPORATION
International Copyright Secured All Rights Reserved

Visit Hal Leonard Online at
www.halleonard.com

Contact us:
Hal Leonard
7777 West Bluemound Road
Milwaukee, WI 53213
Email: info@halleonard.com

In Europe, contact:
Hal Leonard Europe Limited
42 Wigmore Street
Marylebone, London, W1U 2RN
Email: info@halleonardeurope.com

In Australia, contact:
Hal Leonard Australia Pty. Ltd.
4 Lentara Court
Cheltenham, Victoria, 3192 Australia
Email: info@halleonard.com.au

Introduction

Track 1

Welcome to *Play Banjo Today!* This beginner's book will guide you step by step to playing songs on your banjo in the popular and exciting bluegrass style.

About the Audio & Video

All the music written in this book is also on the audio. Each audio example has a track number that appears in the book next to the written music. Check out bonus Tracks 96 and 97 to hear a full performance of the banjo classic "Cripple Creek." Listening to the songs is so important that it actually counts as practice! When you can hear the song in your mind's ear, it will make learning it from the written music easier, faster, and more enjoyable.

Some lessons in the book include video, so you can see and hear the material being taught. Audio and videos are indicated with icons.

 Audio Icon    Video Icon

About the Author

Author Colin O'Brien travels throughout the U.S.A. performing concerts and presenting banjo workshops. He has won several awards for his solo concerts and recordings which feature his banjo, fiddle, guitar, and his amazing foot percussion. He'd love to hear from you! *www.colingobrien.com*

Contents

Meet the Banjo

Track 2

The first banjos in America were brought from Africa in the late 1600s. They were made from gourds and animal hides. These banjos could be considered the great-grandfathers of the banjo you have. Though the African banjos were very different from the one you're learning to play, you'll still see some similarities: the round body covered with a skin, and the neck and strings attached at the back of the body.

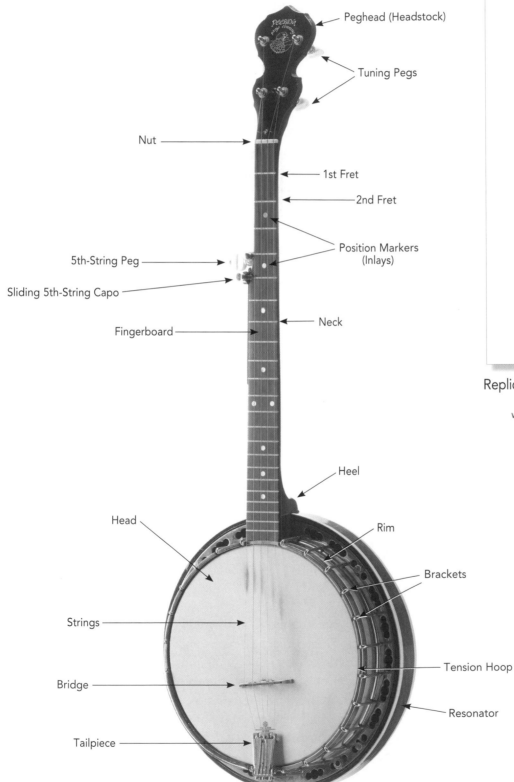

Replica of African Gourd Banjo
(made by Mike Gregory,
www.littlebanjos.lunare.net)

Peghead (Headstock)

Tuning Pegs

Nut

1st Fret

2nd Fret

Position Markers
(Inlays)

5th-String Peg

Sliding 5th-String Capo

Fingerboard

Neck

Heel

Head

Rim

Brackets

Strings

Tension Hoop

Bridge

Resonator

Tailpiece

How to Hold Your Banjo

The Strap

Even if you're sitting, it's very important to have a strap! There are straps made for banjos, but in most cases a guitar strap will work just fine. If you are using a guitar strap, you'll need to tie it onto the bracket hooks at the location shown.

Sitting

Sitting is the most comfortable position when first learning to play. Most of the weight of the banjo can rest in your lap. The strap should be pulled tight over your left shoulder (if you're playing right-handed) so there's no slack in the strap between where it leaves your shoulder and the banjo. This will prevent the neck from sliding down from its own weight. You should be able to sit with no hands on your banjo with the strap keeping the peghead about shoulder height.

Standing

Most players adjust their straps so that the bridge of the banjo is about belly-button height.

Puttin' on the Picks

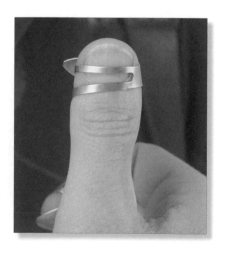

To play banjo in the three-finger bluegrass picking style you'll need two *finger picks* and a *thumb pick*. Thumb picks come in small, medium, and large sizes and are made of plastic or metal (metal pick shown). You'll find that if you try on three plastic thumb picks labeled the same size at a music store, they'll all feel a little different. Try a bunch on until you find one that fits just snug enough to not slip around your thumb when you push on the tip of the pick, which is the part that will be contacting the string when you play. Metal thumb picks can be bent to fit.

Metal finger picks come in one size and need to be bent to fit comfortably around your index and middle fingers. Many players bend the tips back too, so they curve around the tip of the finger. On the finger picks you'll see a number that tells you the *thickness* of the metal. Start with a .15 or .18-size finger pick.

It will take some time for you to get used to the feeling of having picks on. Make sure they are *comfortable*. Everyone's fingers are different, so bend those finger picks around until you find the right shape for your fingers.

Right- and Left-Hand Position

We'll use the terms "pick hand" and "fret hand" throughout this book to accommodate right- and left-handed-players. Left-handed players will need to think of the pictures as if they were looking in a mirror instead of at another player.

Pick Hand

Pick-hand fingers are identified as follows:

T = Thumb
I = Index
M = Middle

The ring finger or pinky (or both) should always lightly rest on the banjo head. This will help stabilize the pick hand when it is picking the strings. Remember to keep both hands relaxed. When playing, both hands are curved as they would be when holding an orange.

Picking closer to the bridge gives you a crisper sound, and picking toward where the neck meets the body gives you a mellower sound.

Fretting Hand

Fret-hand fingers are usually identified by the numbers 1 through 4.

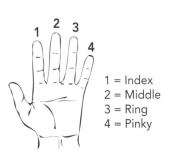

1 = Index
2 = Middle
3 = Ring
4 = Pinky

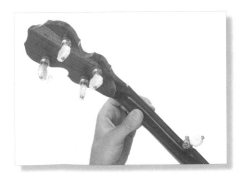

The fret-hand thumb should rest on the center of the back of the neck, as if you're giving a thumb-print.

Your fret-hand fingertips are what touch the strings.

This is a picture of what not to do: don't wrap your hand around the neck like it's a baseball bat. Make sure not to mash your palm against the bottom of the neck.

Make sure there's always room for a pencil to fit between the neck and your palm.

Tuning

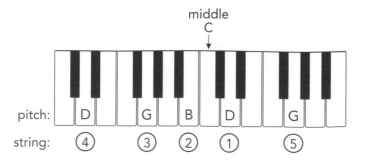

Track 3

Tuning to the Audio

Tuning to the notes on the track is a great way to teach your ears to find the right notes. When you can tell the string you're tuning on your banjo sounds different in pitch from the string played on the track, your ears are doing their job. The next step is to ask; does your note sound higher or lower than the note on the track? If you can't tell, tune the string lower until you're certain it's too low, and then tune it higher until it sounds like the note on the track. This is tuning "up to" the note. After all, we tend to say "let's tune up!" and not "let's tune down." Strings tuned up to the correct pitch will stay in tune longer than if you were to tune down to the pitch.

G Tuning

The G tuning is the most common tuning used for three-finger picking. Strings are tuned to the pitches G–D–G–B–D, and are numbered 5–4–3–2–1.

String 1 is closest to the floor. Strings should be tuned from the lowest in pitch to the highest, meaning you'll start with string 4. On the track at 1:40, you'll hear the strings played in this order:

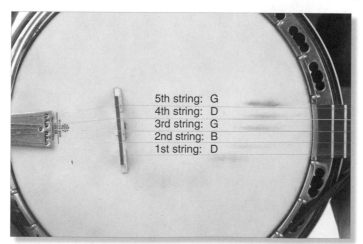

5th string: G
4th string: D
3rd string: G
2nd string: B
1st string: D

- Fourth string, D. This is the thickest string.

- Third string, G.

- Second string, B.

- First string, D. This one is closest to the floor.

- Fifth string, G. This is the short string.

Tuning to a Piano

You can also tune your banjo using a piano. This is similar to tuning to the audio. If your piano has foot pedals, find the pedal that makes the piano notes continue ringing after you strike them; this way you can tune the banjo to the ringing piano note. Like tuning to the audio, this is tuning *by ear*.

middle C

pitch: D G B D G
string: ④ ③ ② ① ⑤

Using an Electronic Tuner

Electronic tuners are available at most music stores. Using a tuner lets you see when you're in tune. Get one to use as your number 2 tuning tool. What's your number 1 tuning tool? Your ears! If you try tuning to a piano or the audio and simply can't get it to sound right, *then* use your tuner, and it will show you whether a string is flat (too low) or sharp (too high). Listen while using it and learn from what it tells you!

Relative Tuning

If you're stuck on a desert island with nothing but an out-of-tune banjo, you can still tune it! Here's how:

1. Tune the 4th string (the low D, the thickest string) to a piano, pitch pipe, electronic tuner, or the audio. If none of these are available, approximate D as best you can.

2. Press the 4th string at the 5th fret. This is G. Tune the open 3rd string to this pitch.

3. Press the 3rd string at the 4th fret. This is B. Tune the open 2nd string to this pitch.

4. Press the 2nd string at the 3rd fret. This is D. Tune the open first string to this pitch.

5. Press the 1st string down at the 5th fret. This is G. Tune the open 5th string (short string) to this pitch.

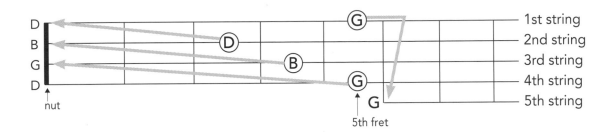

Tuning Tips

*   Always play the string just before turning its tuning peg. This way you'll be able to hear the change in pitch as you're turning the peg.

*   Be sure to turn the peg slowly so you can concentrate on the changes in pitch.

*   Always tune *up to pitch* from below. If it is too high, first tune down past the target pitch.

*   Whatever method you use to tune, it's important to listen. With experience, your ears will become your most reliable tuners. They're very portable, and hard to forget!

How to Read Tablature

Track 4

The five lines you see here are called **tab staff lines**. Each represents one of your banjo strings. The line on the bottom is the short G string. The next line up is the D string, the thickest string on the banjo. The middle line is the second G string. The next is the B string, and finally, the top line is the second D string, which is the string closest to the floor.

Below you'll see some numbers on the staff lines. They tell you which fret and which string to press down with your fretting hand. Occasionally throughout this book you'll also see numbers above the staff lines, as shown in the examples below. These numbers tell you which *fret-hand* finger to use to play that note.

Here you put your index finger on the first fret of the B string.

▶ Notice in all of the pictures that the fingers play just behind the fret, though we use the word "on." This is the area where you'll get the best tone with the smallest effort. This is where you should always play!

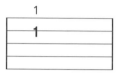

Here you put your third finger on the second fret of the D string.

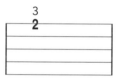

This note is on the thick D string. The second finger goes on the second fret.

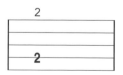

Rhythm

Rhythm tells you two things about notes: when to play them, and how long they last.

Quarter Notes

The staff below is divided into three **measures**. In this book, each measure contains four **beats**. In each measure below there are four **quarter notes**, indicated by a vertical **stem**. Each quarter note lasts for one beat. Just like there are four quarters to a dollar, four quarter notes can fit into a measure. Play the notes below (all are on the middle G string) with your pick-hand thumb, indicated here and throughout the book by a "T" below the note. Your thumb picks in a downward motion. Keep your pinky and ring fingers touching the head as you pick to help you get even rhythm and tone.

Track 5

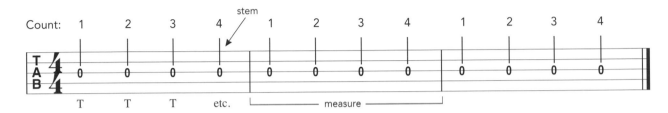

► Playing with a smooth, even rhythm is very important!

Eighth Notes

The most common note value in banjo music is the **eighth note**, designated by the **beams** connecting the stems into groups of four notes. Eight eighth notes fit into each measure. Below are three measures filled with eighth notes. Play these notes on the G string with your pick-hand thumb and count "1 and 2 and 3 and 4 and" as you play.

Track 6

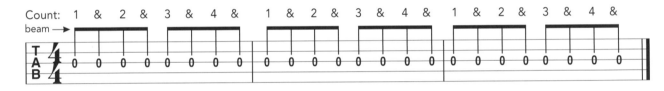

Whole Notes

You will occasionally see **whole notes**, usually at the end of a piece. In rhythmic tablature, we write whole notes with just one fret number in the measure. Like their name implies, they take up a whole measure. Count "one, two, three, four" aloud, plucking the string on beat one and letting it ring for the full four beats.

Track 7

Reading Exercises

The exercises below are played with the thumb (T), index finger (I), and middle finger (M).

This first short exercise is to be played with the thumb. The count written above the staff will help you keep an even rhythm. Count aloud as you play.

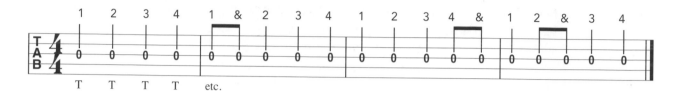

Now it's time to get the pick-hand fingers in on the act. The fingers pick in an upward motion. 90% of the fingers' motion happens from the middle knuckle of the finger. Be sure to keep your pinky or middle finger resting on the banjo head.

Picking the B String: Setup   Picking the B String: Follow Through

Play the following notes with your index finger. Keep the hand nice and steady.

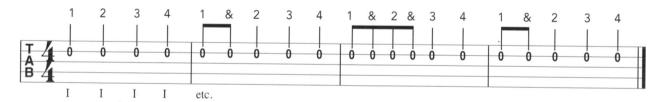

This one on the high D string is to be played with the middle finger.

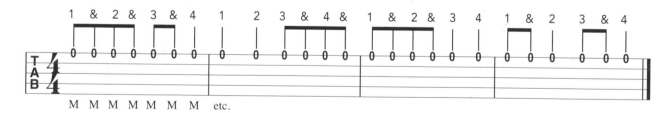

Here's one using all of the picking fingers.

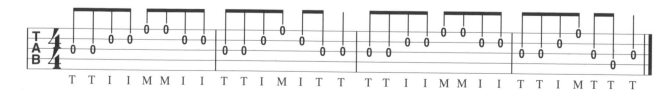

Pinching & Chord Basics

A *pinch* involves picking two or three notes at the same time. Be careful not to pull the pinky and/ or ring finger away from the banjo head when executing a pinch. Listen to the audio to hear the simultaneous notes.

Thumbin' the Gs

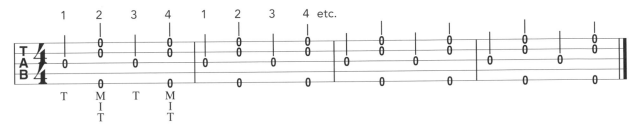

This is the same thing, but now the thumb plays the low D string.

Thumbin' the Low D

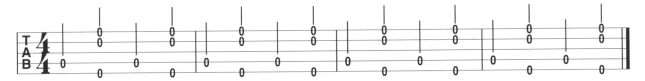

Now the thumb alternates between the G and D strings—hence the title.

Switch Hittin' (Alternating Thumb)

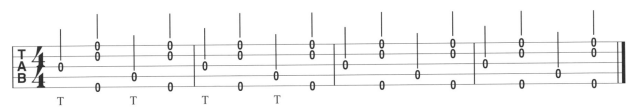

Here's one leading with the index finger. Notice the pinches now only have two notes in them, not three.

Index in the Lead

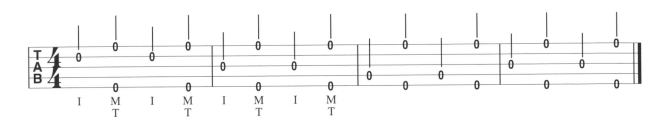

Open-Position Chords

With just three chords, G, C, and D7, you can play many songs on the banjo. The banjo is already tuned to a G chord, so you don't even need your fretting hand for that one! Here are the G, C, and D7 chords in what's called *open position*, the lowest possible position for these chords, which includes at least one open string. The fret-hand fingers are shown beneath the **chord frame**, a type of diagram used for stringed instruments. The thick line across the top represents the nut of the banjo. The chords are also shown in tablature form. When playing the G chord, the fretting hand is like a baseball player waiting for the pitch. It's ready to play with the fingers always curved toward the strings. Strum the chords with the thumb. The thumb brushes toward the floor. Don't strum the short G string on the D7 chord.

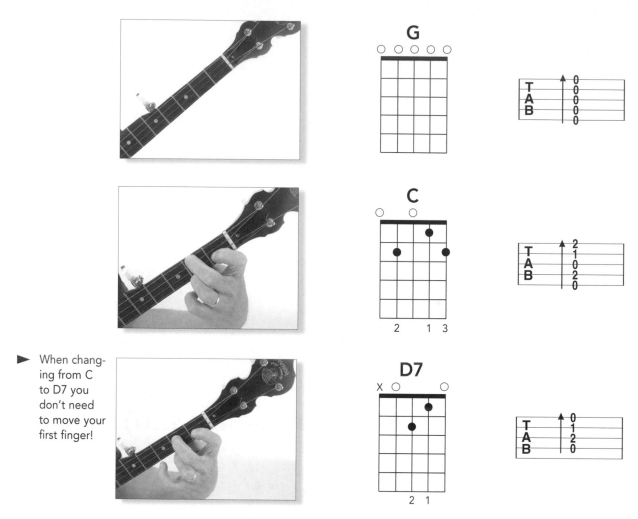

► When changing from C to D7 you don't need to move your first finger!

Now it's time to play some tunes! Here are a few using the pinch you learned.

Notice the direction in the first measure to play the pinch with the thumb, index, and middle finger. The same fingering applies for all the pinches. The last measure of the tune contains **half notes**. Each one of these notes lasts for two beats; the first note is played on beat 1, and the pinch after it is played on beat 3 of the last measure. Count "one, two" for the first half note and "three, four" for the second stack of three.

Track 18

Hello Banjo

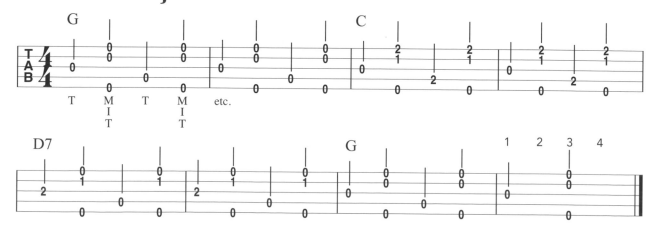

Track 19

Playing Melodies

The *melody* is what you sing or whistle walking down the street, and it's also what you want to hear when playing the banjo. In the next song, the words are under the melody notes.

Goodnight Ladies

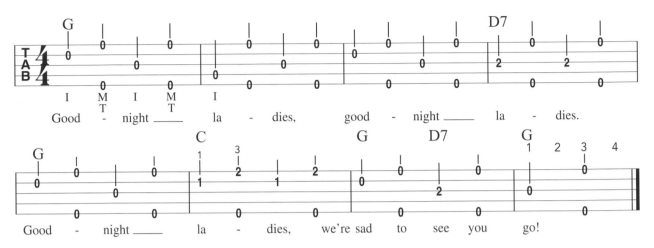

Fingering Tip

When you see a chord symbol such as C or D7, hold the full chord down with the fret hand, even if some of those notes are not supposed to be plucked.

In this tune, you play on the 3rd fret for the first time. The numbers above the staff indicate fret-hand fingering: 1 for index, 2 for middle, 3 for ring finger, and 4 for pinky.

Track 20

Frère Jacques (Are You Sleeping?)

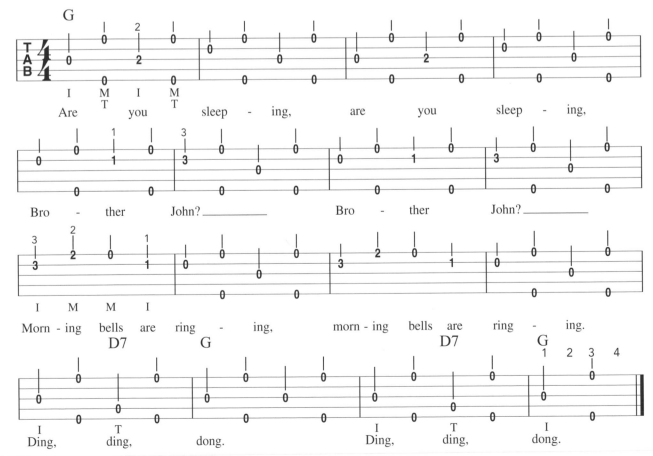

13

Rolls & Slides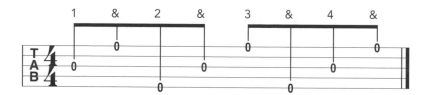

Forward Roll

Bluegrass banjo playing is made up of *rolls*. Rolls are patterns for the picking hand. Your first roll is the *forward roll*. Below is one measure of the forward roll pattern. As you can see it's written using eighth notes, with eight notes fitting into a four-beat measure.

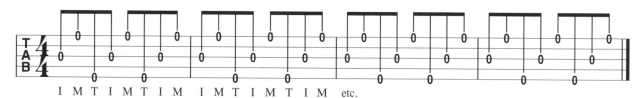

Here are four measures of the forward roll. Play them slowly and be extra careful to keep the rhythm smooth. Try to make it sound like a flowing river of notes. It will help to listen to the track and try to copy the sound.

Track 21

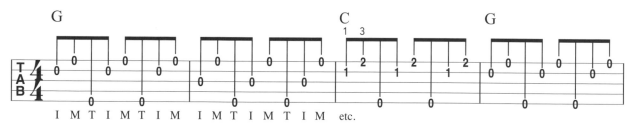

This time the index finger plays the B string instead of the G.

Track 22

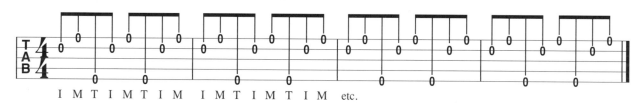

Now it's time for your first song using the forward roll! Again, when you see the C and D7 written above the staff, be sure to hold down the full chord with your fret hand, even if you're not playing all the notes in the chord.

Track 23

Rollin' Forward

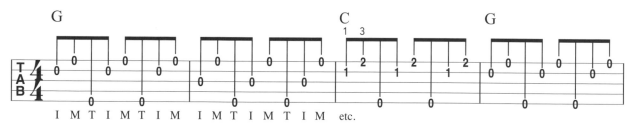

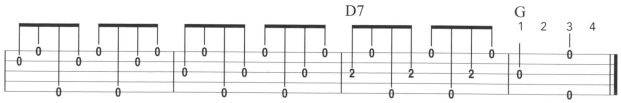

Our next song has been enjoyed by all kinds of people for well over 150 years! The tune combines the forward roll and pinches, eighth notes, and quarter notes. As usual, remember to hold down the entire C and D7 chords when they come up, even though not all their notes may be played. Be sure to see those quarter notes coming in measures 2, 4, 6, and 8, and let them ring for their full beat.

Track 24

Boil Those Cabbage Down

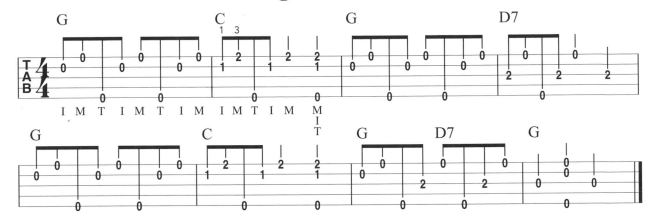

In "Red River Valley," the index finger plays the melody notes (the 1st, 4th, and 7th notes in most measures). To bring the melody out, be sure to let each of those notes ring as long as possible. If it's a fretted note, keep that fret-hand finger down until you play another note on that string. If it's a note on an open string then let it ring until you need to fret that string for another note.

Pickup Notes

A musical phrase may start on a beat other than the first one in a measure. When this happens at the beginning of a song like the one below, it is called a **pickup measure**. Count 1 and 2 silently, and play the first two notes on beats 3 and 4.

Track 25

Red River Valley

► Hold down the full shapes for the C and D7 chords when they come up.

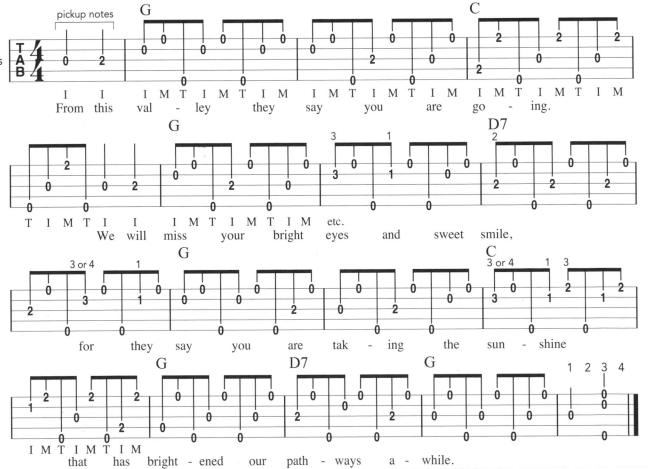

Music History

Also known as "Boil Them Cabbage Down," "Bile Dem Cabbage Down, or "Bake Them Hotcakes Down," this classic American folk song has unclear origins. Folklorist Alan Lomax asserts that the tune has roots reaching all the way to the African slaves brought to the southern United States.

The song "Red River Valley" is one of the most widespread of North American folk songs. Its melody has been traced back to a ditty from the state of New York, "The Bright Mohawk Valley," which was published in 1896. The Red River Valley in this tune is likely the northern one found in Manitoba, Canada.

Track 26

Inside-Outside Roll

Now it's time to add a new pick-hand roll to the mix. The name *inside-outside* describes the picking pattern. Pick two of the inside strings, and then the two outside strings on your banjo. To get the pattern in your mind it may help to say "inside, outside" in rhythm as you play the measures below.

Track 27

I Got the GBGD'S

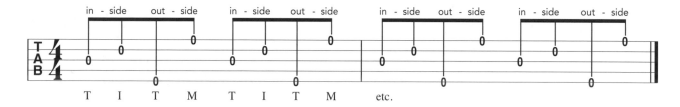

Here is the same pattern, with the thumb playing the low D string.

Track 28

Now I Got the DBGD'S!

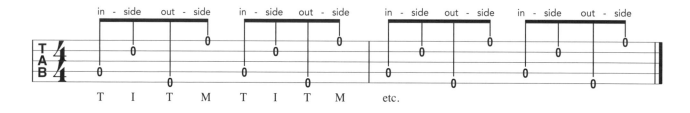

Now try a combination of the two inside-outside rolls.

Track 29

Inside-Outside Combo

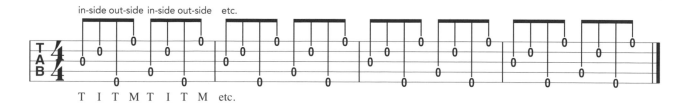

Let's put this new roll to work! We'll start with a tune we learned before, "Goodnight Ladies," which we played with pinches only. Adding the roll gives it more rhythmic interest.

Make sure you pay attention to the "2" above the staff in the first measure. Fret that note with the 2nd finger of the fret hand. When the finger lets go of the note, keep it close to the string, ready to play. Watch the right hand in measure 6; you're holding two strings down at the 5th fret.

Track 30

Goodnight Ladies
(with Inside-Outside Roll)

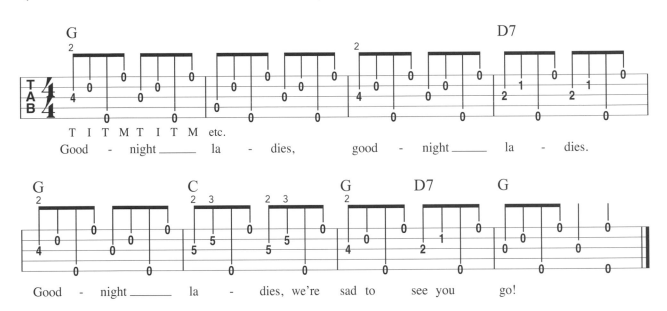

The different rolls work together to create a variety of sounds all in the same tune. Variation makes a tune more enjoyable to both play and hear. This tune combines the forward roll and the inside-outside roll.

Track 31

Go Tell Aunt Rhody

► Practice the 2nd measure as a round (over and over in rhythm) to get used to starting the forward roll with the thumb.

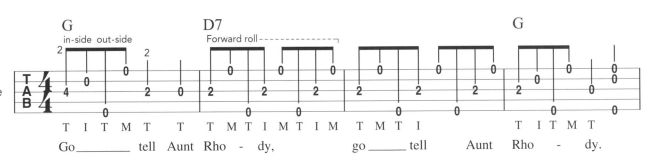

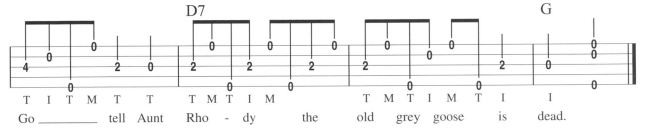

Measure Numbers

Sometimes a composer (or a teacher) will put **measure numbers** on the music to make it easy to point out which ones need practice. The pickup measure, if there is one, is usually not counted in the numbering scheme.

Practice measure 3 alone, and when it feels smooth, play measures 2 and 3 together as a "round"— over and over with no break in the rhythm.

Track 32

Will the Circle Be Unbroken

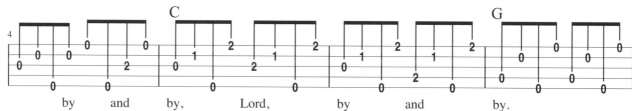

In measure 6, hold down the C chord and move the second finger only for the fifth note in that measure.

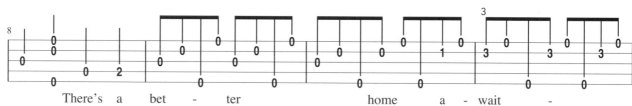

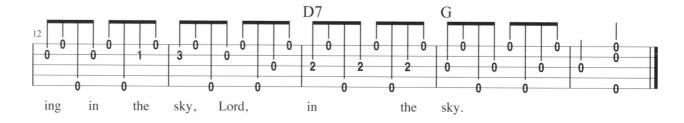

Track 33

The Slide

Of all banjo techniques, *slides* perhaps come closest to mimicking the human voice. They are a powerful tool for bringing variation to a tune. Slides are sounded by the fret hand without being picked, and are indicated in music by lines between the notes. Sometimes you'll also see an *sl* under the line.

When playing the following measures, only pick the string on beats 1, 2, 3, and 4. The notes on the "ands" are created by the fret-hand slide. All slides in the following examples are played with the 2nd finger of the fret hand. These need to sound as even eighth notes. As you count "1 and 2 and 3 and 4 and," slide when you say "and." Be sure to listen to the track.

18

Track 34

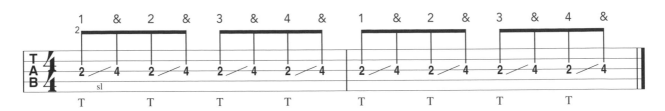

Now let's put slides into the inside-outside roll. The slide is the same as above, but now you also play the open B string at the end of your slide, on the "and." Play slowly and try to make the slide and the open note sound at the same time.

Track 35

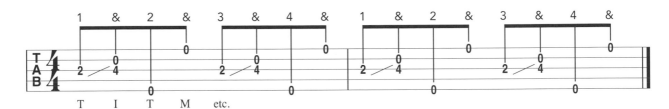

Track 36

Goodnight Ladies
(Using Inside-Outside Roll, Pinches, and Slides)

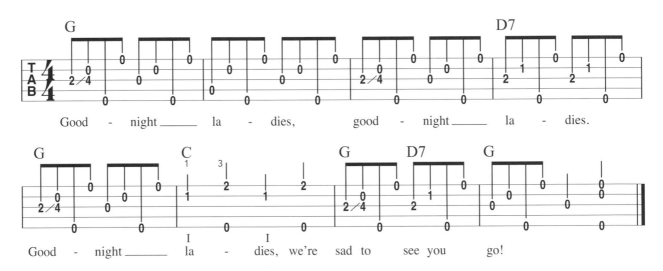

Here is a three-fret slide on the low D string, from the 2nd to the 5th fret. As in previous examples, make sure you're sliding in an even, steady rhythm. Be sure not to speed up. As you count "1 and 2 and 3 and 4 and," pick the string on beats 1, 2, 3, and 4. Slide (without picking) when you say "and."

Track 37

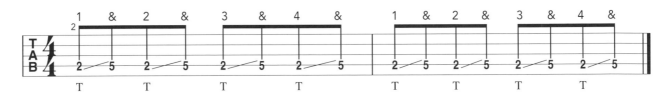

Now practice the sliding lick for the next tune by itself.

Track 38

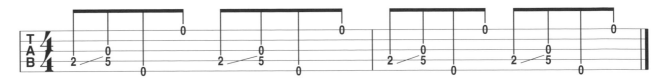

She'll Be Comin' 'Round the Mountain

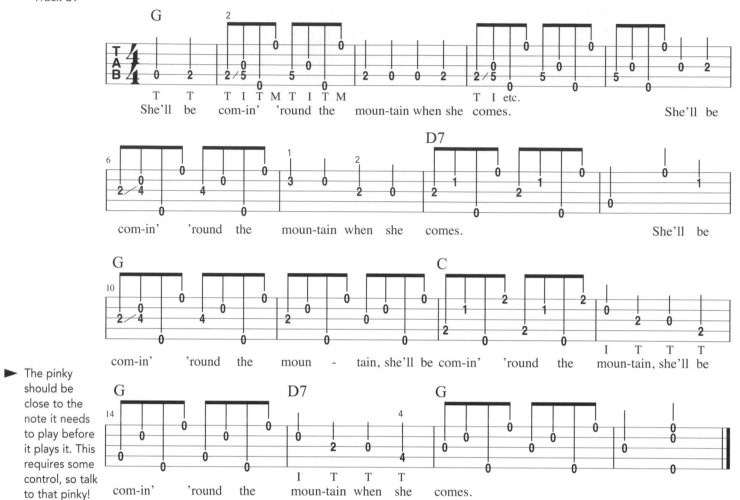

► The pinky should be close to the note it needs to play before it plays it. This requires some control, so talk to that pinky!

Repeat Signs and Numbered Endings

Repeat signs are double barlines with two dots, as shown in measures 1 and 4 of the next tune. Just as the name implies, repeat signs tell you to play certain passages twice. The brackets above the final two measures indicate *first* and *second endings* to the repeated section.

Here's what you do:

- Play the first line up to the repeat sign at the end of measure 4 (the first ending).

- Without missing a beat, go back to the first repeat sign at the beginning of measure 1.

- Play the first three measures, *skip measure 4*, and play measure 5 instead.

- Keep going, to the next line in this case.

"Old McDonald" combines the inside-outside roll, slides, pinches, and some single notes. Notice that some of the slides go from fret 2 to 4, while others go all the way from the 2nd to the 5th fret. The fourth measure has a little bass run on the D string. Note the fret-hand fingering. Listen closely to the track to get the timing of the slides right.

Old McDonald

Track 40

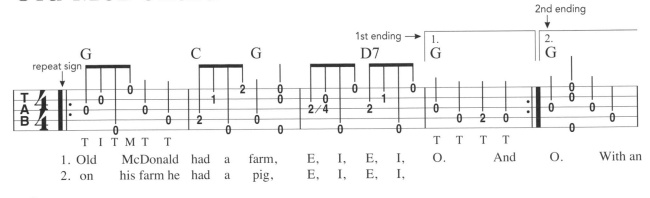

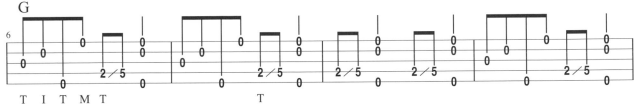

T I T M T T   T T T T

1. Old   McDonald had a farm, E, I, E, I, O.   And O.   With an

2. on   his farm he had a pig, E, I, E, I,

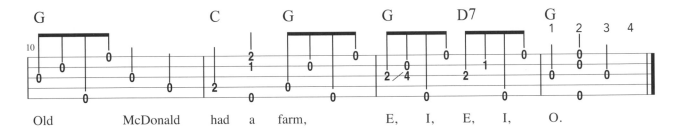

T I T M T   T

oink, oink here, and an oink, oink there,   and here an oink, there an oink, ev'ry-where an oink, oink.

Old   McDonald   had   a   farm,   E, I, E, I,   O.

Music History

Like most folk songs, "Old McDonald" has parents. According to Mr. Doney Hammondtree, it likely came from an older song called "The Merry Green Fields of the Lowland" (Vince Randolph, Ozark Folksongs Vol. 3 No. 457) which he learned in 1900. The earliest official publication of "Old McDonald" is 1917, when it appeared in a book called *Tommy's Tunes*.

Our next picking pattern is the ***forward-reverse roll***.

Forward-Reverse Roll

Track 41

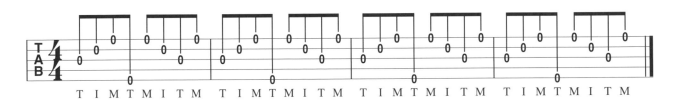

T I M T M I T M   T I M T M I T M   T I M T M I T M   T I M T M I T M

The following tune uses the forward-reverse roll all the way through to the last measure. Hold down the whole C and D7 chords. In measure 14, lift your index finger for the open B string.

Worried Man Blues

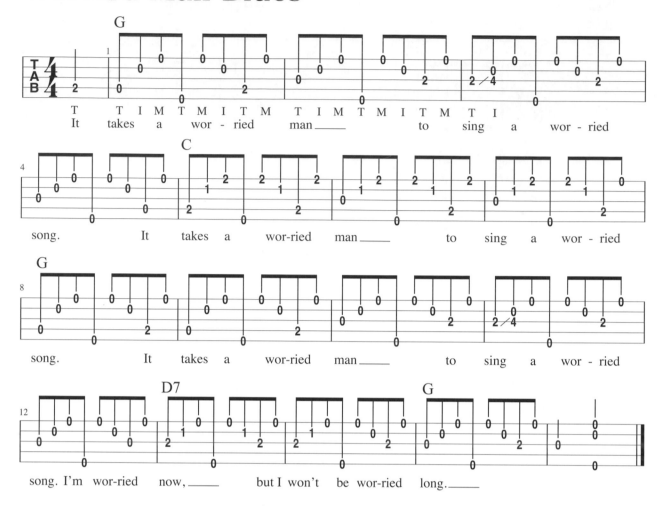

Music History

"Worried Man Blues" has become a standard in roots music repertoires, but its exact origins are lost in the mists of nineteenth-century folk music. Its famous opening line, "It takes a worried man to sing a worried song," was popularized on records in 1930 when the Carter Family recorded it. Lester Flatt and Earl Scruggs recorded it in 1961.

This version of "Go Tell Aunt Rhody" combines the forward-reverse roll with slides and pinches.

Go Tell Aunt Rhody

► In the 7th measure, keep the whole D7 chord pressed down, just lifting your index finger for the open B string note.

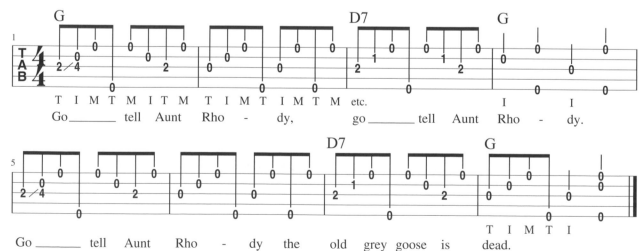

Pickin' a Classic

"Cripple Creek" starts with a pickup note on beat 4 that is slid into beat 1 of the first measure. Rehearse this slide as a repeating loop all by itself, counting aloud in even rhythm. Pick the note on beat 4 and slide it when you count beat 1: "1 2 3 pick, slide 2 3 pick, slide 2 3 pick, slide 2 3 pick, slide." Slide with your third finger on the D string. Notice the final slide goes over the repeat sign; it means that last note in measure 4 slides into the first measure. Match your sound to the track. Once you play this, you're dipping a couple toes into Cripple Creek for sure!

"Cripple Creek" Slide

Track 44

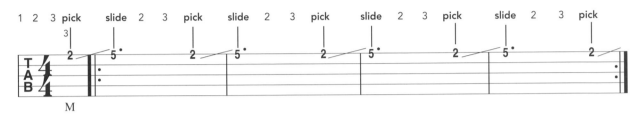

Measure 2 of "Cripple Creek" contains a forward-roll and pinch combination. Practice it until you can play it smoothly, and you're waist-deep in Cripple Creek at least!

Track 45

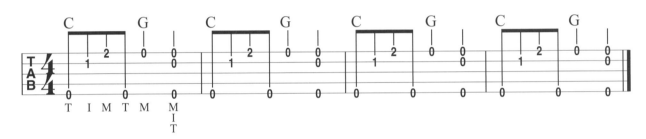

"Cripple Creek" originated as a fiddle tune. It has an "A" part (the first line) and a "B" part (the second line). Both parts are played twice. To end the tune, play the 1st ending of the "B" part. "Cripple Creek" is perhaps the single most popular tune to pick on the five-string banjo.

Cripple Creek

Track 46

▶ The 2nd ending of the "B" part is only played if you're continuing back to the "A" part. Play the 1st ending of the "B" part on the second time through the "B" part to end the tune.

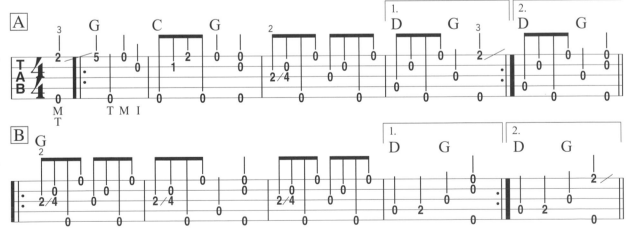

In the fourth and fifth measures of each section, there is a D chord indicated in the music, but you do not make a D chord here. All the strings are open. If someone were playing rhythm for you, that's where they would play a D.

Hammer-Ons

Track 47

In playing the banjo, some notes can be sounded by the fret hand without being picked, such as the slides you learned earlier. The second technique to work on for this is called the *hammer-on*.

Start with proper fret-hand position, keeping your thumb behind the neck. Pluck the open G string.

Hammer with the middle finger, *just behind* the fret. Hammer so that if the banjo neck weren't there, you'd hammer your finger straight into your thumb.

When you release the finger, keep it close to the strings (within 3/4 of an inch), as it needs to be ready to play again.

The key to clear hammer-ons is not strength. If you hammer straight into the fretboard and accurately (just behind the fret), you'll have strength to spare and get a nice-sounding hammered note.

A hammer-on is written with a curved *slur* mark. The thumb picks just the first note. The second is sounded by the fret-hand hammer-on.

slur

It's Hammer Time!

Track 48

On the G string:

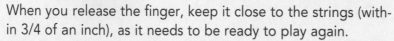

T   T   T   T   etc.

Try them on the D string:

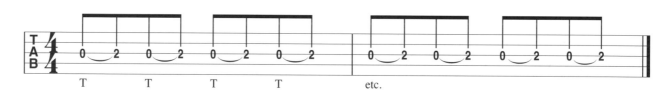

T   T   T   T   etc.

Now play the same hammer-ons, but add a picked note with the index finger. This note is played at the same time as you hammer. Picking one note while hammering another may feel strange at first, but go slowly and you'll get it!

Track 49

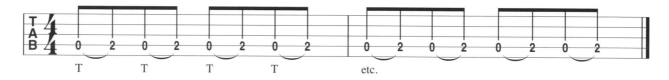

24

Practice hammer-ons with the inside-outside roll. Keep a steady rhythm.

Track 50

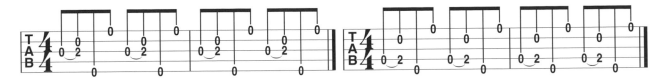

Now let's try "Cripple Creek" with some hammer-ons. To end the tune, play the 1st ending of the "B" part like on page 23.

Track 51

Cripple Creek

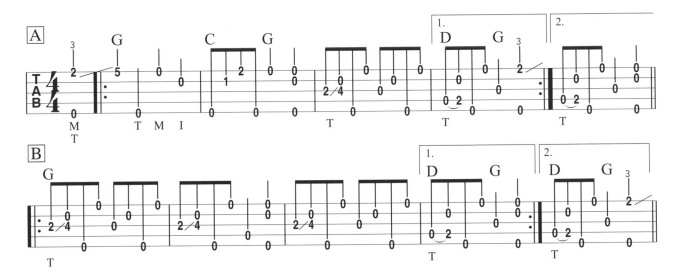

Track 52

Pull-Offs

A *pull-off* is another way for the fret hand to sound notes. Starting from a fretted note, the fret-hand finger flicks the string as it comes off, either pulling slightly toward the floor or pushing toward the ceiling. Practice it both ways. Either way, the sound of the lower note comes when the finger releases the string.

Play each of the following measures several times in a row in a nice steady rhythm.

Pull (down) and push (up) the G string.

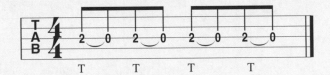

Now pull and push that big D string.

Pull-offs and hammer-ons are both marked with curved slurs in the music.

Pull-off in a Roll
(with a Pinch and a Slide)

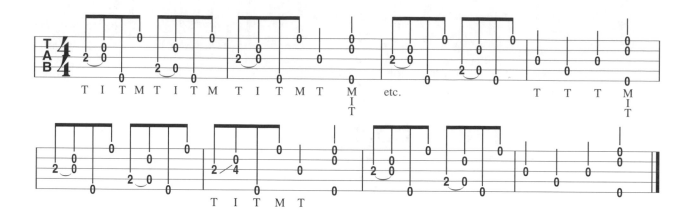

Here's a familiar song worked up with slides, hammer-ons, and pull-offs. As you can see, each hammered note is the second eighth note in a group of four. Hold down the hammered note while the rest of the notes in the group are played. For example, the hammer-on in the first measure is held down until you get to the first note of the second measure. In measure 14, after the slide, be sure to hold down the 2nd finger (on the 2nd fret) while the pinky plays its note on the 4th fret of the low D string.

She'll Be Comin' 'Round the Mountain

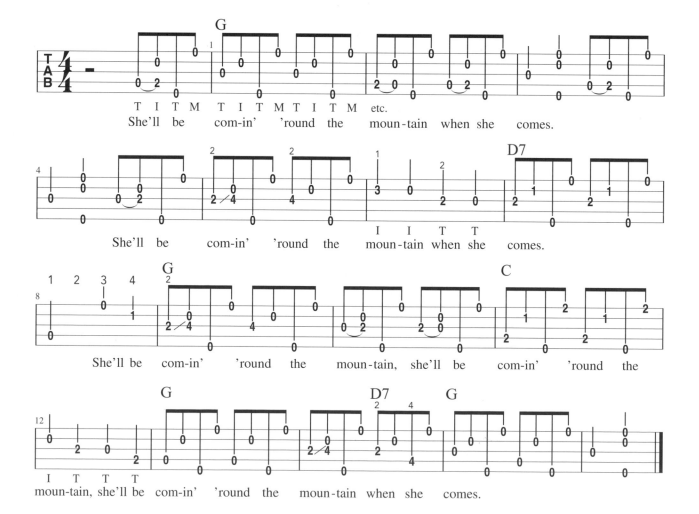

A Big Lick

Track 55

This quintessential Earl Scruggs bluegrass banjo lick, once learned, can be used again and again in countless tunes! It's one of the ABCs of bluegrass banjo. Before trying the lick, first play this exercise, picking the high D string as you slide. Remember to count "1 and 2 and 3 and 4 and" and slide when you say "and."

▶ Take your time, and make sure you use the correct picking-hand fingers!

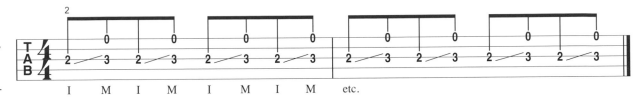

This version of "She'll Be Comin' Round the Mountain" uses our new lick in measure 3, and also mixes in some different rolls. The Scruggs lick also appears as a nice ending in measure 15. In measure 7, we insert a forward-reverse roll for the D7. In measure 14, the two notes after the slide are both held down until the first note of the next measure.

She'll Be Comin' 'Round the Mountain

Track 56

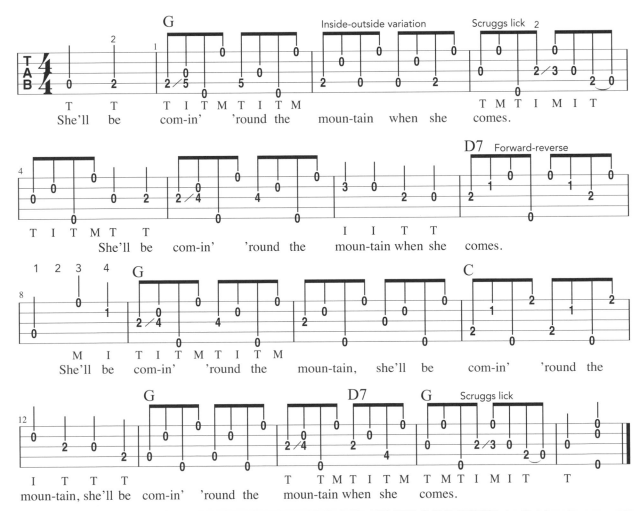

To get the feel for the picking in measure 12 of "Walkin' Cane," play these pretty notes several times.

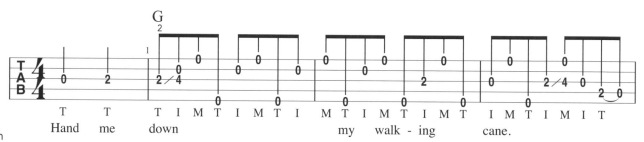

Watch the picking for the Scruggs lick; it starts with the index finger. In measure 6, there's a variation on the forward roll. It's similar to measure 2 in "Will the Circle Be Unbroken." In that same measure, notice the first note is picked with the thumb.

Walkin' Cane

Track 58

▶ The slide in the Scruggs licks in this arrangement slides all the way to the 4th fret instead of the 3rd. Compare the different sounds between the two!

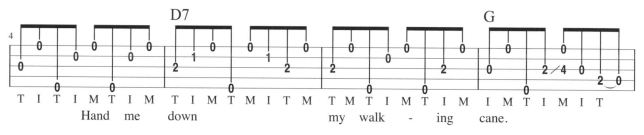

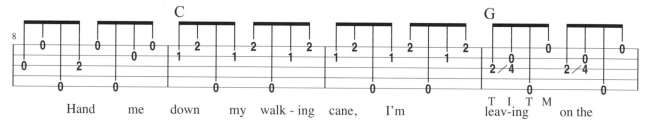

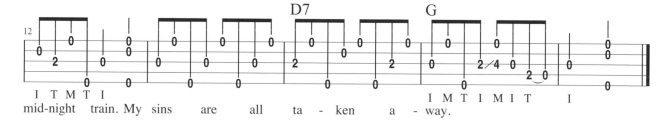

Music History

Gid Tanner and His Skillet Lickers first recorded "Hand Me Down My Walking Cane" in 1926. Gid Tanner was one of the most widely-recognized names among country music enthusiasts of the 1920s and 1930s, and the Skillet Lickers were one of the most influential string bands during the formative years of the country music industry.

Lesson 6 | Note Names

The musical alphabet uses seven letters, from A–G, to name notes and chords. The lowest note on the banjo is the 4th-string D, with the other letters following in alphabetical order up the neck, until you reach another D note at the 12th fret. At that fret, the series starts over.

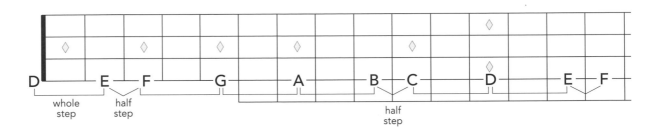

Most of the letters are two frets apart. This distance is called a **whole step**. From E to F, and from B to C, we have **half steps**, notes that are only one fret apart. This fact means that it's not necessary to memorize the name of the every note on the neck right away. Just start by remembering the names of the open strings, and that B–C and E–F are half steps, one fret apart.

The unlabeled notes are named by using the words **sharp** (♯) or **flat** (♭) in relation to the note immediately below or above. For example, the first fret on the string may either be called **D♯**, because it is a half step above D, or **E♭**, because it is a half step below E. Which name is correct depends on the scale or key the note is used in at the time. For now, we can name these notes either way.

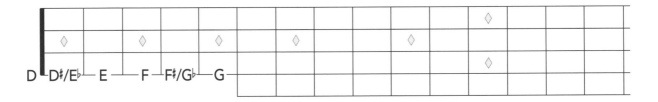

The alphabet starts from G on the 3rd string, again with half steps from B–C and E–F, reaching another G at the 12th fret.

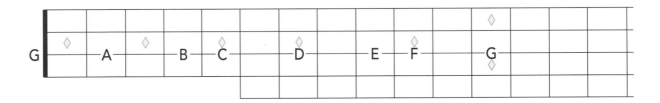

The B string goes up to another B at the 12th fret, with a C right on fret 1. That's the **root** of our C chord.

The 1st string is an open D note, the same pitch as found on the 12th fret of string 4. Its notes are the same as on the 4th string, but an **octave** (eight letters) higher.

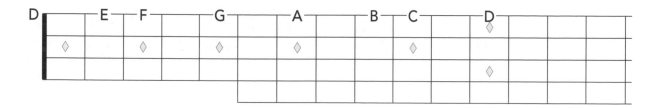

The short G string is the same as the 1st string from fret 5 up. Advanced banjoists make use of this knowledge as they play high up on the neck. As beginners, we're only using this string as an open **drone** note, the characteristic banjo sound.

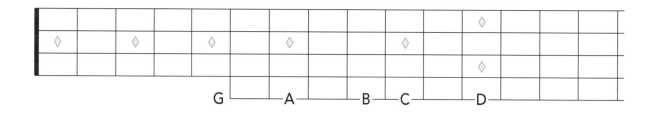

It will help to be familiar with note names for the next lesson on chords, so review this section a few times before then.

Track 59

A New Hammer-On

Thus far, all of the hammer-ons you've played have been from an open string to a fretted note. Now we will hammer from one fretted note to another. Start with your index finger on the second fret.
Keep it down throughout. Pick this note, then hammer on with the second finger. Hammer just behind the fret as always. Alternate between picking the starting note with your index finger and thumb as indicated.

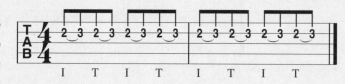

Now we'll add the open D string. Hammer the B string just as you pick the D string; not before.

Now play this complete phrase several times with even rhythm. We owe Earl Scruggs a big thanks for this popular hammer-on lick.

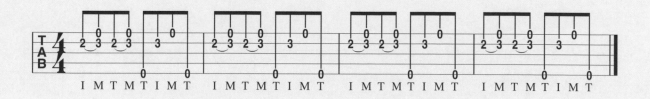

30

In the next tune, watch for the quarter notes in measures 4 and 5—no running stop signs! In measure 6, from the D7 chord move the 2nd finger only for the note on the low D string.

Train 45

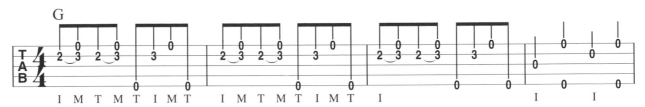

► All the notes in the last line are fretted with the 2nd finger.

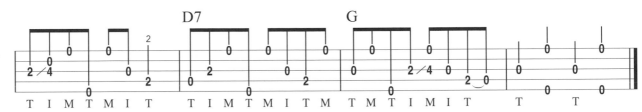

In "Goin' Down That Road Feelin' Bad," the pickup measure is a classic *lead-in* starting on beat 2. Besides starting tunes, it can start solos or *breaks* within tunes. This tune also includes your first *double tag* ending. This ending can be used to end other tunes as well.

Goin' Down That Road Feelin' Bad

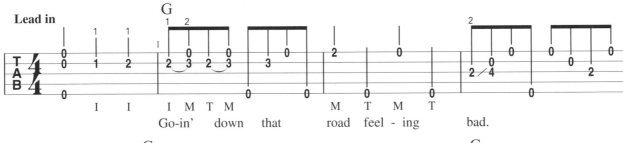

► In measures 5–6 and 9–10, move only your second finger for the note change during the C chord. Leave all other fingers down.

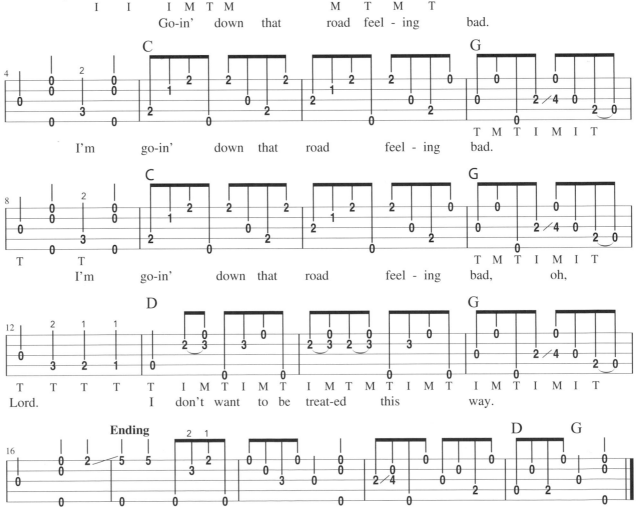

Major Chords

Track 62

If you look at individual musicians in any ensemble, be it a bluegrass, rock, or jazz band, you'll find that each player spends the majority of time playing a supporting, or **backup** part. In rock music it may be called playing rhythm, which backs up the lead. When someone is singing or when someone else is playing a solo, the banjoist often backs them up with the chords for the song.

We've learned three chords thus far: G, C, and D7. We've learned them in open position, where each chord uses some open (unfretted) strings. (The G chord actually uses all open strings!) Now it's time to learn to play **major chords** (those represented by a letter name only) in closed position. As the name implies, there are no open strings when playing closed-position chords. These are essential to playing basic backup rhythm.

Learn Your FDAs (Banjo Vitamins)

There are only three closed major chord shapes on the banjo. Each of these three shapes is moveable to anyplace on the neck. Where a shape is played determines the name of the chord. In the diagrams below, the root note of each chord shape is circled. As you learn each shape, focus on the root so that you'll know which chord (A, B, C, etc.) the shape is producing when played at a particular fret.

First, we have the **F shape**, named after the chord this shape produces when played at the third fret, with the root under the ring finger. This is a new shape for us, using all four fret-hand fingers. A closed-position G major chord using the F shape is shown here. The root is played by your ring finger on fret 5. Play the chord, then lift all your fingers to check that it sounds similar to the open-position G chord that you already know (the one with the open strings). Move this same shape up towards the banjo head by two frets, and you're now playing an A chord.

Thumb Test

As you practice, give each chord the **thumb test**. Hold down the chord shape and pick each string with the thumb, one at a time. If a note sounds muted or if it buzzes, look at the fretting hand and find the finger responsible for that note. Is it correctly placed on the right string and pressing down sufficiently? If the answer is "yes," and there's still a problem, then perhaps another finger is leaning into (and muting) the problem string. Keep the fingers arched!

► Move it down to the third fret, and it's an F major chord.

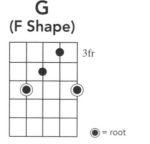

G
(F Shape)

◉ = root

Next is the **D shape**. It's named after the chord the shape produces when played at the fourth fret, with the root on the 2nd string, fret 3. Here is a closed-position D chord using the D shape.

► This D chord becomes an E chord if you move it up two frets.

D
(D Shape)

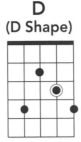

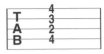

Finally, there's the **A shape**, named after the closed-position, second-fret A chord (also called the *barre* shape). Here is a closed-position C chord using the A shape. The root is on the 3rd string. Keep the finger straight and check that all the tones ring. No bent bar here!

► This shape becomes a D chord if you move it up to the 7th fret.

C
(A Shape)

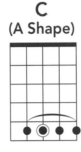

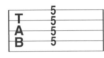

Play each of these chord shapes in various places on the neck and hear the huge variety of sounds just three shapes can make! To name the various chords, remember (and listen for) which note in the shape is the chord root, and if necessary, review **Lesson 6—Note Names**.

Once you get the hang of each chord shape it's time get that pick hand involved. The measures below show one of the most common pick-hand patterns for backup (also called *accompaniment*), using the open G chord.

Track 63

Backup Pattern

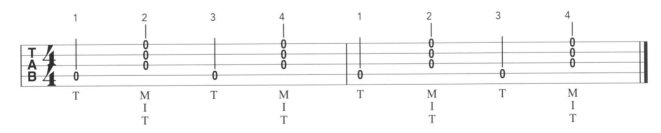

The next step is to hold each closed-position chord shape down while picking this pattern. Play each measure several times.

G (F shape)   D (D shape)   C (A shape)

Track 64

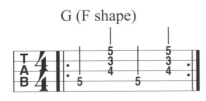

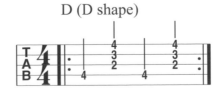

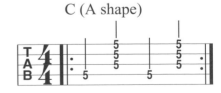

33

Changing Chords

When changing from G to D, the index and middle fingers exchange strings: the index goes to the middle finger's string and the middle finger goes to the index finger's string. Focus your attention on either finger and visualize where it needs to go, and the other finger will move to its new home naturally.

Let's practice this part of the chord move alone. We'll call this part the *flip*. Play this *very slowly*. The pinky and ring fingers stay on their same strings. Don't lift them at all.

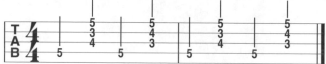

For the complete chord change, just relax the grip and slide the hand down one fret. You're not going for the sound of a slide here, just economy of motion. The movement of fingers as you change from chord to chord should be as efficient as possible. Don't lift a finger more than is necessary.

Now add this slide before the flip. Play slowly. Repeat.

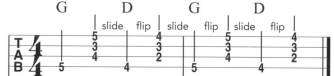

Here's another tip to smooth out the chord change: you needn't plant all the fingers at once. The first note for each chord is played by itself, so you can flip the fingers during the time that note is being played. Pluck the chord, then loosen the grip as you slide to the next low note and press it down. Then flip the others into place.

Now let's practice the change from G to C. While holding your hand on the G chord, focus on your index finger only. Visualize its move up to the 5th fret for the A-shape C. Conversely, when you're playing the C chord, have the ring finger in your mind, as it's the first finger you'll need to put down when returning to G.

You can plant the other fingers to complete the G chord while the ring-finger note is being played. You don't need to lay the whole G chord down at once.

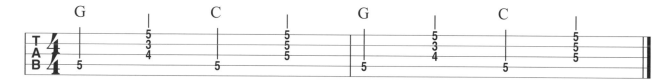

Backup Accents

There are four beats to each measure for everything in this book. This is called a *4/4 time signature*. Beats 1 and 3 are downbeats, and beats 2 and 4 are called *upbeats*. When playing backup it's usually a good idea to play louder on (or **accent**) the upbeats. In the following example, the pinches in the backup pattern are on the upbeats, so you play those a bit louder. However, you can't play louder than the singer or soloist, as your job is to support them.

Muting

A good way to create accents and have your playing heard in the proper way is to **mute** the strings. This gives the sound a nice punch, or pop, and prevents the strings from ringing too loudly. After you play the pinch part of your backup picking pattern, relax the fretting-hand fingers so they're barely touching the strings. This stops the strings from ringing. Pick the strings, then let up the pressure to mute. Listen to the track and try to imitate its sound.

Goodnight Ladies Backup

Track 67

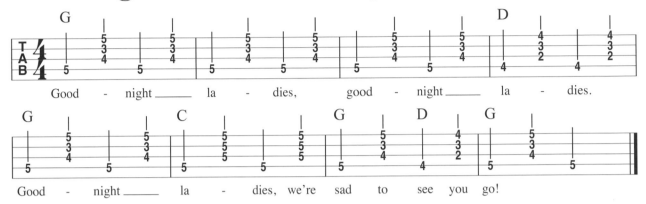

Good - night ____ la - dies, good - night ____ la - dies.

Good - night ____ la - dies, we're sad to see you go!

Reading Chord Charts

Throughout this book there are chord names (G, C, D7) written in the music. These have two functions:

1. They tell you which open-position chord to hold down with the fret hand when playing the arrangements of the songs.

2. They also tell you which closed-position shapes to use for playing a backup part to the songs. Instead of reading the notes given on the staff, count your way through the measures and play the given chord using the backup picking pattern. This is using the music as a **chord chart**.

Here's a chord chart for "Cripple Creek." Only the chord names are written. You have to count! There are four beats per measure, which in your pattern equals thumb, pinch, thumb, pinch.

Notice the 2nd and 4th measures have a chord change in the middle. Change chords on beat 3. Use the slide-and-flip technique for the change in measure 4. All other chords change on the first beat.

Cripple Creek Chord Chart

Track 68

► When reading a chart, look ahead to see what chord is coming so you'll be ready for it.

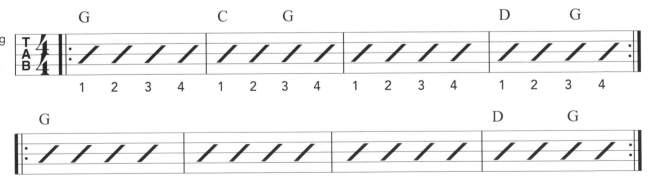

Now that you know the basic backup pattern, you can practice backing up all the tunes on the audio! When you read the tunes as chord charts, you'll notice a D7 chord is often used, as that's the position your fret hand needs to be in when playing the written lead part. When playing backup, however, use the closed-position D chord we learned when you see a D7 in the music.

Sixteenth-Note Licks

The new aspect to this slide lick is that the slide itself is faster. It's written in **sixteenth notes**. Two sixteenth notes equal the duration of an eighth note. Listen to the example, and keep your foot tapping the same steady quarter-note beat as always when imitating it.

In tablature we have fret numbers instead of the noteheads used in standard notation.

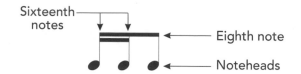

Be sure to start your slide just behind the 2nd fret. Dig in a little bit and be sure you can hear the sound of the finger sliding over the 2nd fret.

Track 69

Sixteenth-Note Slides

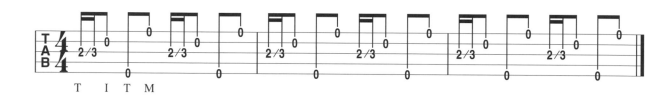

Track 70

A New Pull-Off

Here's a new pull-off lick using sixteenth notes. As with previous pull-offs, practice the licks below two ways: one, pulling off toward the floor, and two, pushing off toward the ceiling.

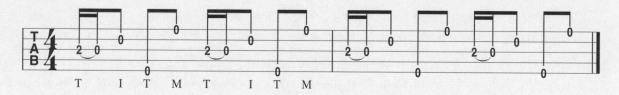

Now combine the sixteenth-note slides and pull-offs.

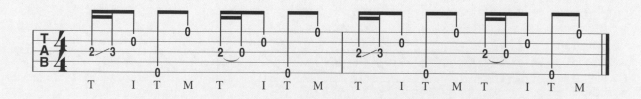

Make sure all the notes (especially the sixteenths) are clearly audible. How should they sound? Listen to the track!

Once you get the hang of these licks, you're ready for a full-blown Earl Scruggs version of "Cripple Creek." This is full-steam-ahead bluegrass!

End the tune by playing the 1st ending of the "B" part, like in the other versions of "Cripple Creek" in this book.

Cripple Creek

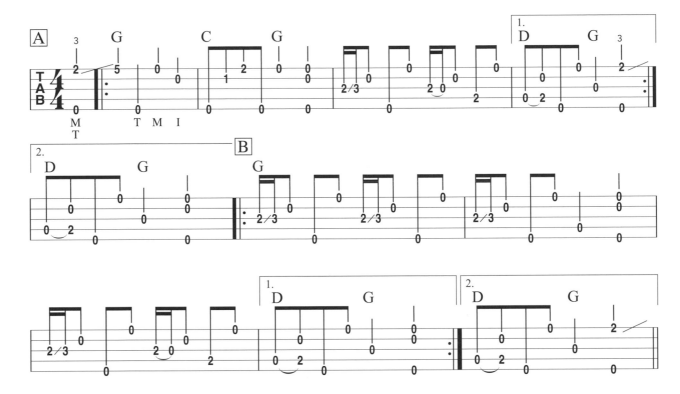

Pullin' Off a New Pull-Off

Let's get ready for the next lick by practicing pull-offs to a fretted note instead of an open string. Keep the index finger down, and make sure you play a smooth rhythm of even eighth notes.

Now we'll play the fretted pull-offs as sixteenth notes, as part of a roll. Be sure the index finger is down by the time you pull off.

Nine-Pound Hammer
(Puttin' in the Pull-Off)

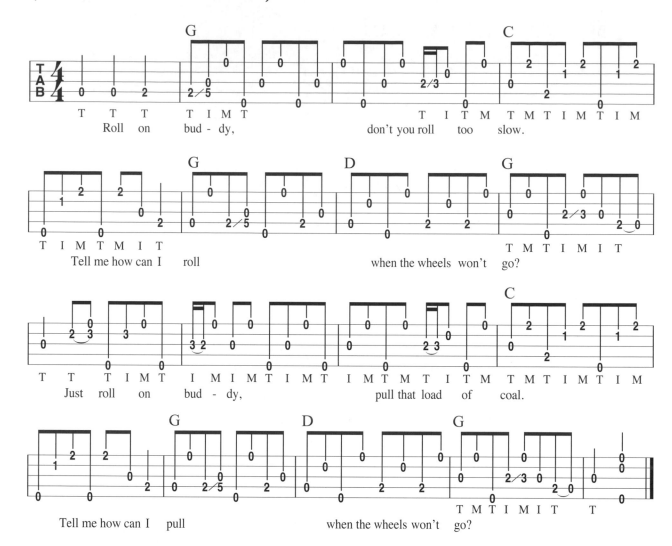

Roll on bud-dy, don't you roll too slow.

Tell me how can I roll when the wheels won't go?

Just roll on bud-dy, pull that load of coal.

Tell me how can I pull when the wheels won't go?

The Banjo Language

When we talk, we use inflection in our voices, and can choose among many combinations of words that express our ideas in a way that fits any mood or situation. This we do without needing to think about it, because we are fluent in the language. This same idea applies to music and to banjo playing. You now have in your banjo vocabulary some different pick-hand patterns and fret-hand techniques. The key to becoming fluent with them is to use them!

The Capo

A *capo* is a good friend to the banjo player, especially those who play in the blue-grass style. It raises the pitch of the open strings. Most guitar capos will work on a banjo, but it's best to get a banjo capo. They're available at most music stores.

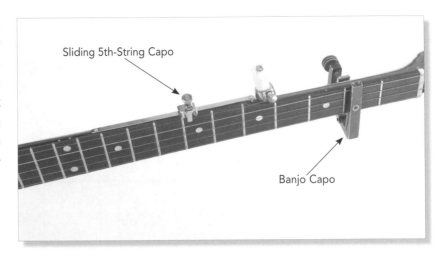

Sliding 5th-String Capo

Banjo Capo

Why Use One?

Capos enable the banjoist to play in different keys without changing their fingering. To be able to play in different keys is essential. For instance, a vocalist may want to sing in the key of C, or a fiddler may want to play a tune in D or A. While the banjo as an instument can accommodate any key, the bluegrass style relies on the effect of open strings. To preserve those open strings in different keys, a capo is at times a necessity.

Track 74

Putting It On

The capo should be put on just behind the fret (the same place you'd put your fingers), and should be snug enough so all the strings sound clear when strummed open. If it's too tight, it will pull the strings out of tune. If it's too loose, the strings will buzz.

Most banjoists have "railroad spikes" installed on the necks of their banjos. These are very small L-shaped hooks behind the 7th, 9th, and sometimes the 10th fret, under the short G string. Hooking the string under one raises its pitch. A qualified individual only should install these! Another solution for the 5th string is a sliding 5th-string capo (as shown in the photo).

If you have a capo, place it at the 2nd fret to play the following tune in A, and hook or capo the short G string at the 7th fret. You can also tune the short string up to A. Though usually played in A, "Old Joe Clark" can also be played in G without a capo.

When reading the tablature, all fretted notes are read in relation to the capo. For example, a "2" means two frets higher than the capo fret, which is now "0." The written G chord will sound as an A.

If you are playing with another instrumentalist, he or she must transpose the chords. A guitarist may use a capo or transpose the music.

"Old Joe Clark" also uses the F chord that the F shape is named after. Slide your familiar closed-position G chord down so that your index finger is at the first fret (relative to the capo) and you have the F chord.

Old Joe Clark

Track 75

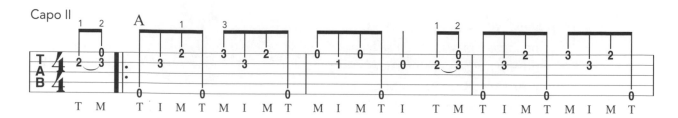

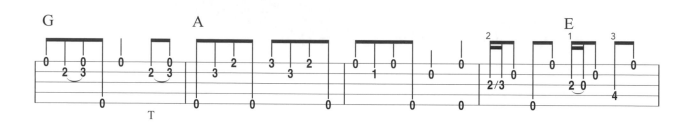

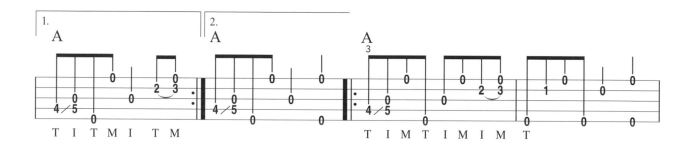

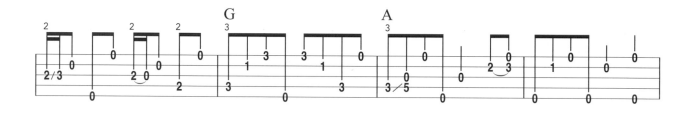

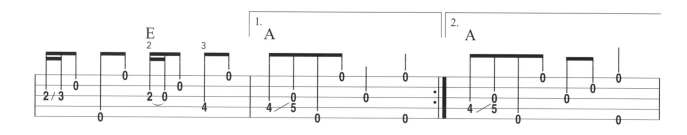

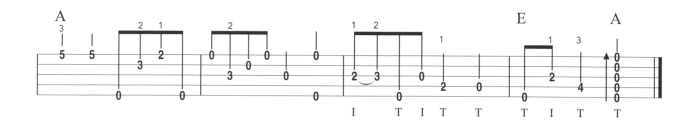

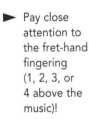

Track 76

Backward Roll

The *backward roll* is the exact reverse of the forward roll.

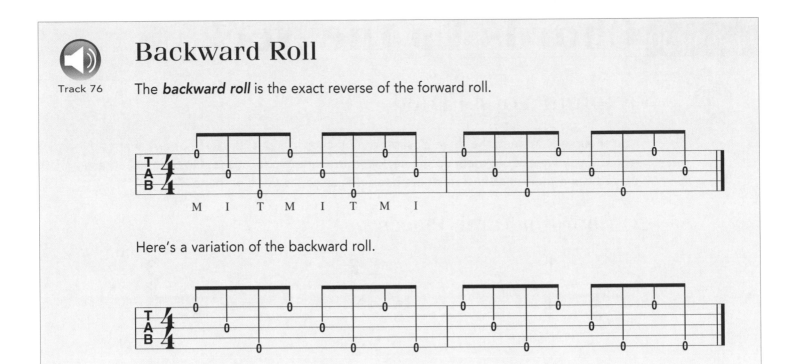

Here's a variation of the backward roll.

Playing Up the Neck

So far, all of your playing has taken place up to the 5th fret, unless you used a capo. As you can well see, there's a whole neck to use. Let's crack it open a bit! The following high break uses the variation of the backward roll and 2nd zone partial chord shapes. We'll talk more about these after you enjoy the following melodious sounds.

Track 77

Boil Those Cabbage Down

► Pay close attention to the fret-hand fingering (1, 2, 3, or 4 above the music)!

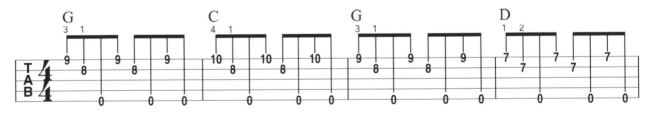

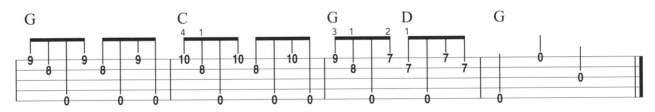

"Boil Those Cabbage Down" sounds pretty as a duet if you have someone else play the low version.

Chords Up the Neck

Track 78

Expand Your FDAs!

You've already learned the three closed-position chord shapes, the F, D, and A shapes. Now it's time to play each of them up the neck in three different locations. On the track, these are played using the thumb test one note at a time, as you learned on page 32.

G Chord in Three Places

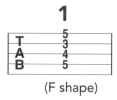 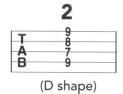 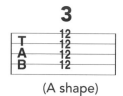

C Chord in Three Places

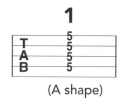 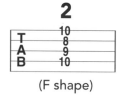 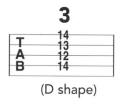

D Chord in Three Places

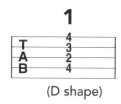 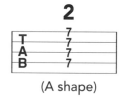 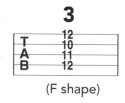

Track 79

Now it's time to play each chord in three places using the backup picking pattern. Take it very slow and try to envision the first note of the next chord before going to it! (They're circled.)

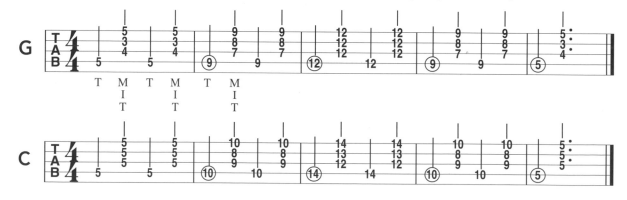

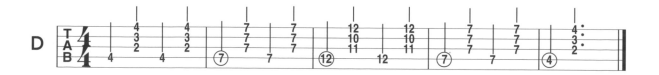

Three Chord Zones

Here's how you can play G–C–D–G in three "zones" on the neck. Notice you use the same three chord shapes in each zone, in a different order, and for a different chord.

Zone One

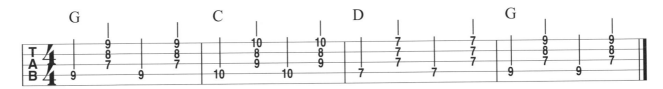

Zone Two

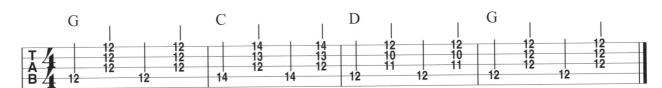

Zone Three

Backup Tips

1. When playing backup say the name of the chord to yourself (or aloud).
2. Play each chord (G, C, and D) in each of its three places on the neck.
3. Play backup using each position. When each position feels somewhat familiar, experiment with combining them. For example, play the progression G–C–D–G like this:

Zone-to-Zone Backup

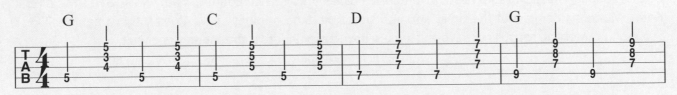

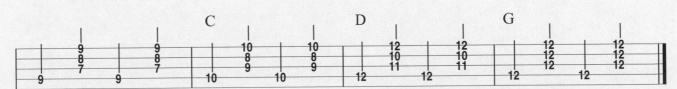

What have you done? You have now played the G, C, and D chords using each closed chord shape!

43

This tune is commonly played in the key of A, with a capo on the 2nd fret. The only full chord you hold down is the F in measure 3 and first half of measure 4. The 2nd finger plays the pull-offs. The other fret-hand fingers (holding down the F chord) don't move. In measure 11, hold down the top two strings of the F chord.

Track 84

Salt River (Salt Creek)

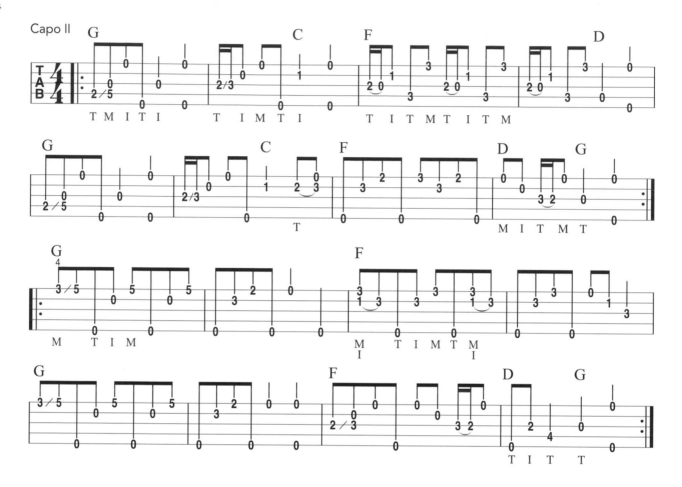

Music History

"Salt River" is an example of how a traditional tune gets a new name, which then gains acceptance through popular use. Old-time players call this fiddle tune by its original name, "Salt River." "Salt River" probably refers to the river by that name in Kentucky. Bill Monroe and His Bluegrass Boys recorded this fiddle tune in 1964 under the title "Salt Creek," in honor of the creek in Indiana near where Monroe held his annual Bean Blossom Festival. Bluegrass pickers have since come to know it as "Salt Creek." Bill Keith, Monroe's banjoist at the time, apparently got the tune originally from West Virginia banjoist Don Stover. The Monroe recording gave this tune a new lease on life in the bluegrass circuit.

Single Eighth Notes

A single eighth note carries a *flag*, compared to the multiple eighth notes we've seen with *beams* joining their stems. Just like each beamed eighth note, a single flagged eighth note lasts for half a beat.

Stem ———→   ←——— Flag

Notehead ———→

In tablature, we have fret numbers instead of the noteheads used in standard notation.

Track 85

Dotted Notes

When you see a *dot* after a note, the duration of that note is increased by one half of its value. A quarter note gets one beat; a dotted quarter gets one and a half beats. When a dotted quarter note starts a measure, the note after it must fall on the *upbeat* (or "and") of 2.

You will rarely see dotted notes in banjo music; however, they'll make an appearance in "Hava Nagila!"

Track 86

C Minor Chord

"Hava Nagila" on the next page uses the C minor chord. It's a close relative of the open-position C major chord you already know. Lower both E notes (on strings 1 and 4) to E-flat at the 1st fret to change C major to C minor. You'll have to flip the 1st and 2nd fingers to switch to this chord from C major. More on minor chords in Lesson 12.

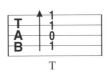

Single-String Picking

This is when you play the same string two or more times in a row. All notes are played with the thumb and index finger. When single-string picking, do not deviate from the T I picking pattern! It will feel strange for a while but you'll get used to it.

So Far Away

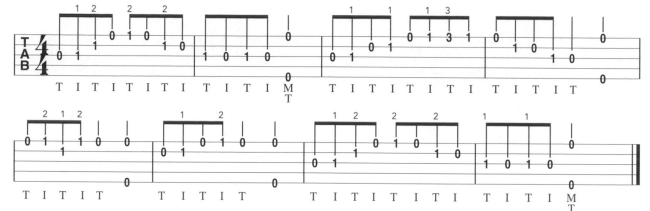

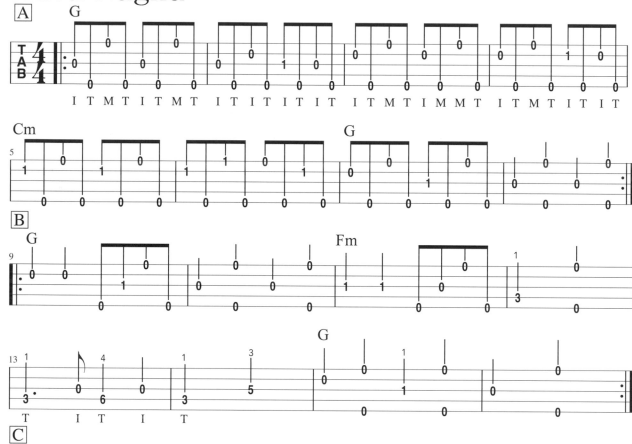

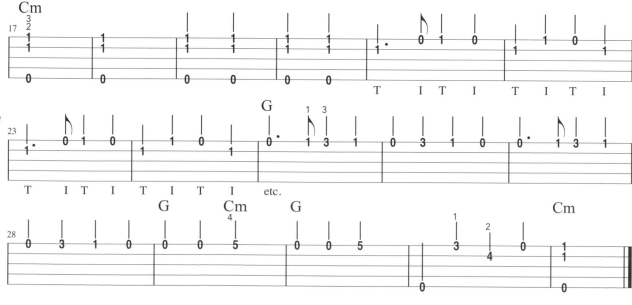

Track 87

► In measures 5 and 6, use the two fret-hand fingers indicated. Don't jump with one finger between strings.

Track 88

Hava Nagila

► In measures 22 and 24, from beat 3 to beat 4 is called "crossing under"; be sure to follow the right-hand fingerings indicated.

46

Lesson 12 | Minor Chords & Major Scales

Minor Chords

The three closed-position chord shapes you've learned are major chords. Major chords become *minor chords* by lowering one note. To change from C major to C minor, we lowered the E's to E-flats. In music theory, the 3rd of the chord is the note that's lowered to change from major to minor. As a beginner, you just need to learn the minor shapes and relate them to the major ones.

The change to minor requires rearranging the fingering of the chords, so be sure to read the fingering given below the diagrams. When you have them fingered correctly, play each one with the muted backup pattern, and try some rolls as well. Although only one note is changed, the minor chord is immediately recognizable and very different-sounding from its major counterpart.

Track 89

Major Chord Shape

Minor Chord Shape

 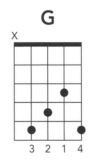

G
X
3 2 1 4

 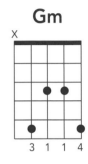

Gm
X
3 1 1 4

C
X
1 1 1 1

Cm
X
2 3 1 4

 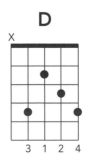

D
X
3 1 2 4

 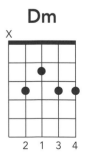

Dm
X
2 1 3 4

Although only one song in this book ("Hava Nagila") uses a minor chord, you'll come across more songs that use them. Some popular tunes that use minor chords are "Shady Grove," "Foggy Mountain Breakdown," "Jerusalem Ridge," and "Devil's Dream."

Major Scales

Scales are the palette from which come melodies. It's a great idea to become acquainted with scales, as they will enhance your overall musicianship. By playing these consistently over time, you'll develop your ear and be able to play a melody by hearing it. You'll also develop dexterity and technique.

G Major Open Position

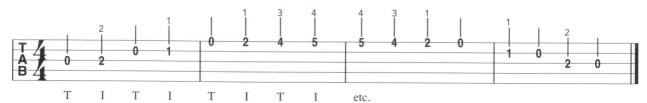

G Major Closed Position 1

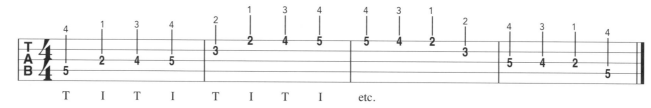

Scale shapes that do not include open strings can be moved to any key. For example, to play an A major scale, start this shape from fret 7.

G Major Closed Position 2

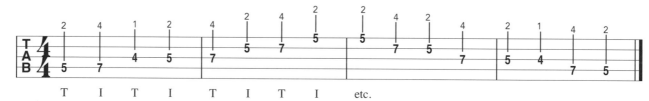

Melodic Style

The bluegrass "filler-note" approach is not used in the melodic (also called "Keith," or *arpa*) style. Rather, each note is more likely to be a melody note. One distinct feature of this style is that the notes are played *across* the strings. No string is played twice in a row, and this is what gives the melodic style a flowing and sometimes harp-like sound. This approach was devised by Bill Keith, whose efforts allowed fingerpicking banjo players to tackle fiddle tunes.

G Major Scale, Melodic Style 1

G Major Scale, Melodic Style 2

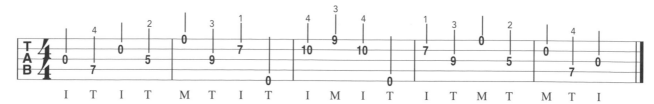

Introduction to Bluegrass

Track 98

This portion of the book is for players already familiar with bluegrass basics. The material presented will include advanced bluegrass as well as melodic style, single-string style, and chord melody. Music theory is presented, applied, and integrated into the lessons throughout the book. The written music in this book is a bridge—it leads you to where the music is. When you fully know a piece, you no longer need to read the music—it is memorized in your mind and your fingers.

The "strike zone" is where a good baseball pitcher throws the ball, and it's also where a banjoist keeps their fingers. It is important to keep the left- and right-hand fingers in the strike zone (close to the strings at all times). The left-hand fingers should stay within about an inch of the strings when they're not fretting notes. If they stray farther away (for instance, the pinky tends to straighten out), it just means they've got farther to travel to get back to the strings! You'll find it easier to execute clean, left-hand techniques (hammer-ons, pull-offs, slides, etc.) with confidence when playing within the strike zone. The strike zone also applies to the right hand; the fingers should always be within about an inch of the strings.

Another subject worthy of attention is the importance of playing steady rhythm. If you're playing with a relaxed, steady, groovy rhythm and you play a wrong note, it will probably be okay—it may even come out sounding like a lick! On the other hand, if you play all the right notes but are lacking a relaxed, rhythmic feel, it's simply not going to be enjoyable to play or listen to. Ultimately, it could be argued that it would be better to play the wrong note at just the right time than it would to play the right note at the wrong time. The *metronome* is a great tool to get the rhythm of your playing together. With every click, it tells you where the beat is in true mathematical time. The goal is not to play like a metronome, but rather cultivate a relaxed relationship with true time. As you become comfortable playing along with the metronome, you'll find it can infuse your practice sessions with a meditative quality. It is also a great tool for organizing your practice sessions. For instance, when you're working on your speed, the metronome tells you at what *tempo* (beats per minute) you are able to play a particular tune or passage. Write that number down, and that's the speed to exceed in your next session.

Bluegrass

Bill Monroe, the father of bluegrass music, began playing professionally in the 1920s. At that time, the banjo was still regarded as a four-string rhythm instrument used in jazz ensembles. It wasn't until 1945, when Monroe gave Earl Scruggs a job, that the banjo became a featured instrument in country music. Monroe's new-sounding music combined the blues and Scotch-Irish influences (fiddle tunes) with an adventurous imagination. The sound of Monroe's group in 1945 came to define what we know of as bluegrass.

The four banjo **breaks** (solos) in this lesson use the bluegrass techniques previously presented in this book: *forward roll, inside-outside roll, forward-reverse roll, pinches, slides, hammer-ons,* and *pull-offs*. These right- and left-hand techniques are freely woven into the arrangements to provide rhythmic interest and to bring out the melody.

Track 99

Playing the Words

"Goin' Down That Road Feelin' Bad," "Nine Pound Hammer," "Will the Circle Be Unbroken," and "Hand Me Down My Walkin' Cane" all are **songs**, which is to say they are sung. When the vocalist sings, they use words, pitch, rhythm, and inflection to express music. The arrangements presented here are instrumental breaks; they can be played as solos between the vocalists' singing. By playing with a steady rhythm and emphasizing the melody notes, you can play the words on your banjo! The lyrics of the following songs are written below their melody notes. These are the notes that should have most emphasis, the other notes being played quieter. The banjo now gets to sing the words with its own voice!

> **Recommended Listening**: Earl Scruggs, John Hartford, Sonny Osborne, J.D. Crowe, and whomever these fine players listen to.

Hammer-On the C Chord

Below you'll see a Click with a snazzy hammer-on. Once memorized (that shouldn't take long!), look at your left hand and make sure that your 2nd finger is hammering just behind the fret and that it never leaves the strike zone. Playing this is not about power, but relaxed accuracy.

Track 100

Hammer in the Sea

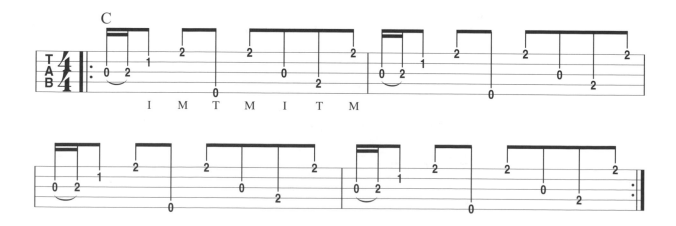

Goin' Down That Road Feelin' Bad

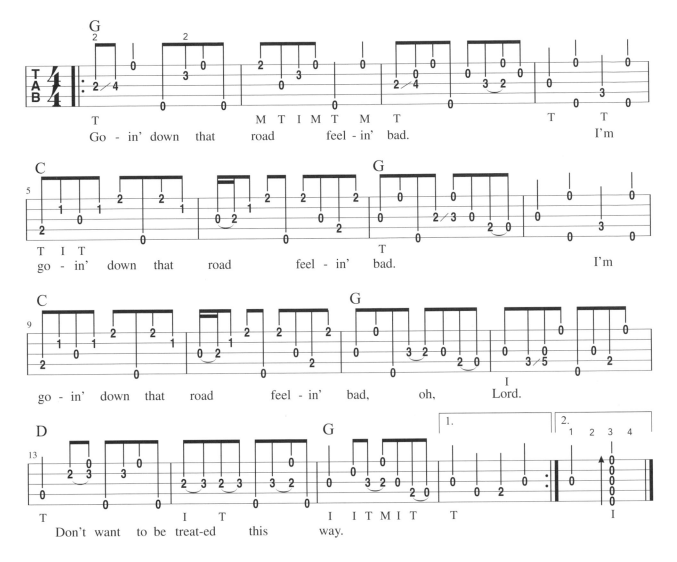

Check out this new pull-off lick. Be sure to keep the 1st finger of the left hand down between pull-offs. Try them two ways: pulling toward the floor or pushing toward the ceiling.

New Pull-Off Lick

► Try these pull-offs in other songs you play as well.

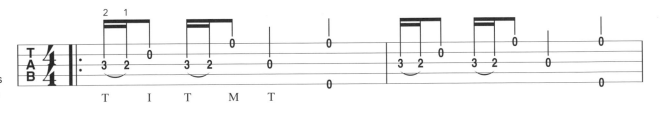

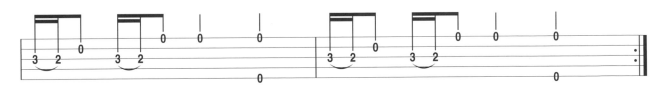

Will the Circle Be Unbroken

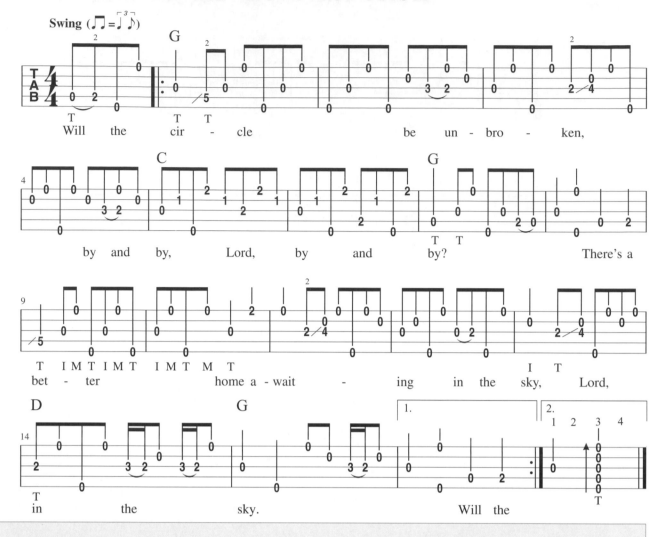

Swing Feel and Triplets

When you listen to "Will the Circle Be Unbroken" you'll be hearing what is called *swing feel*. Swing is a rhythmic feel that is easily heard, but difficult to notate. Other terms used to describe it are "shuffle feel," "dotted feel," or "lilt." Swing could also be described as delaying the upbeats in music. One measure of eighth notes is counted "1 & 2 & 3 & 4 &." The upbeats are the "ands." Play the upbeats a little late without budging the downbeats and you're exploring swing territory.

The next song, "Nine Pound Hammer," uses a new rhythm called a *triplet*. A triplet is three notes, as the name implies. In the next song a triplet appears in measure 7, and it takes up the same rhythmic space as one quarter note, or two eighth notes. A fun way to sing triplets is "sci ba da, di ba da, sci ba da, di ba da!" "Sci ba da" takes up one beat and "di ba da" also takes up one beat. Both triplets and swing underscore an important point: if you want to learn it, listen to it!

Before playing "Nine Pound Hammer," try these hammer-ons and pull-offs on for size. The eighth-note part of this lick (first two beats of each measure) can be used as an alternate lick in some other songs you already know—it fits well in many places!

Pull-Off/Hammer-On Combo

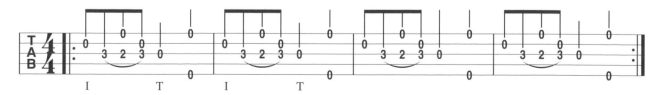

Nine Pound Hammer

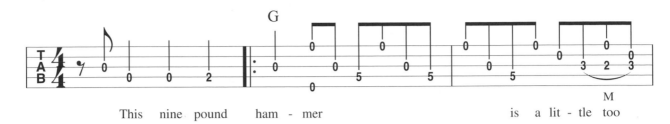

This nine pound ham - mer is a lit - tle too

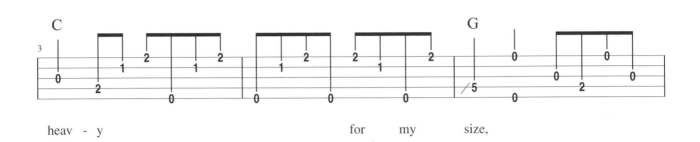

heav - y for my size,

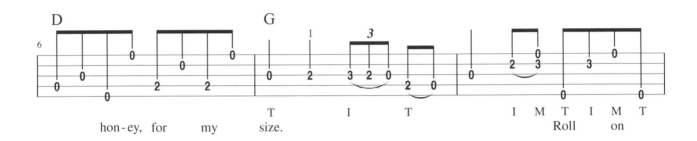

hon - ey, for my size. Roll on

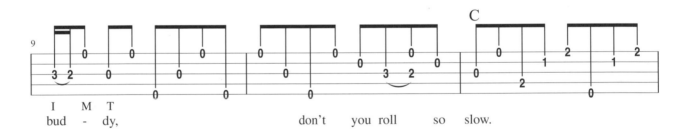

bud - dy, don't you roll so slow.

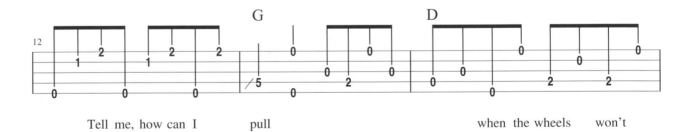

Tell me, how can I pull when the wheels won't

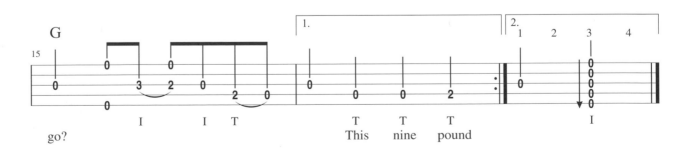

go? This nine pound

The lead-in here lick here is very similar to the one used in "Will the Circle Be Unbroken."

Hand Me Down My Walkin' Cane

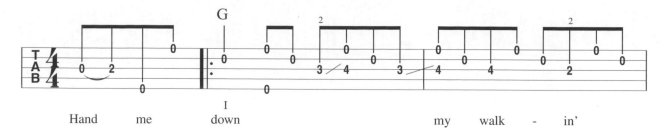

Hand   me   down   my   walk - in'

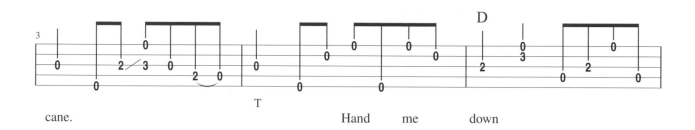

cane.   Hand   me   down

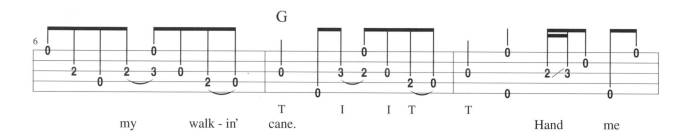

my   walk - in'   cane.   Hand   me

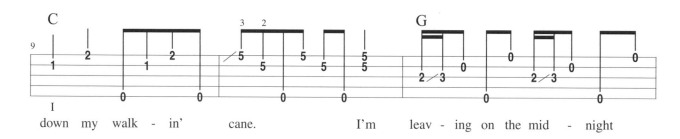

down   my   walk - in'   cane.   I'm   leav - ing on the mid – night

 In measure 11, you'll find a lick right out of "Cripple Creek."

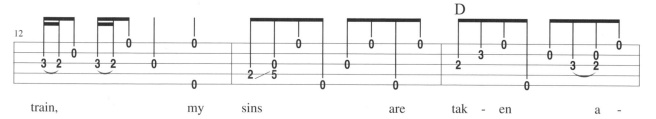

train,   my   sins   are   tak - en   a -

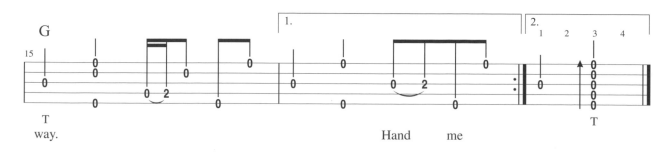

way.   Hand   me

54

Bending

Bending from, Bending to

There are three components to a *bend*: where it starts, where it ends, and what happens in between (the bending note itself). First, make sure you establish the note you're bending from. That is, let the unbent note sound (perhaps for just an instant) and then bend it. When you bend a note, you raise its pitch. The notation shows a curved arrow pointing toward the step value, such as 1/2 (a half step). Here's how that sounds.

Bend Exercise

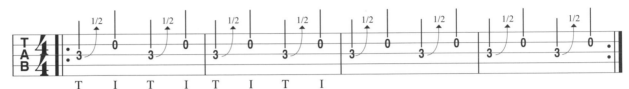

The Flat 3rd or "Blue Note"

If you play the 4th fret of the G string without bending the note you're playing the note B. This is the third note of a G major scale (G–A–**B** or DO–RE–**MI**) and is called a *major 3rd*. Now move the note to the 3rd fret of the G string. This note is B♭ (B flat). You have *flatted* (lowered) the third note of the scale, so it's now called a *flat third* (or *minor 3rd*). This is a highly expressive note! The above Bend Exercise is a good example of the flat 3rd resolving to a major 3rd. In general, flat (minor) 3rds imply tension and major 3rds have a resolved, happy sound. By bending the B♭ (flat 3rd) up toward the B (as in the above exercise), you hear its bluesy, expressive effect. Be sure to listen to the track!

Don't Let Your Deal Go Down

► This song is in the key of F. The chord progression is common in jazz and is known as a VI-II-V-I progression.

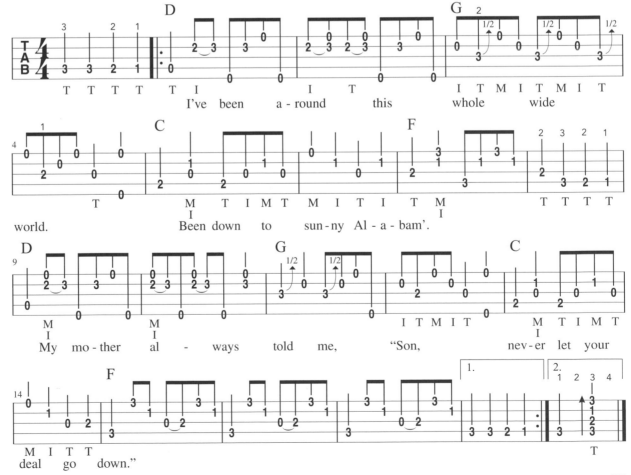

55

Here's how the flat 3rd bend sounds an octave higher up the neck.

Track 110

High-Bend Exercise

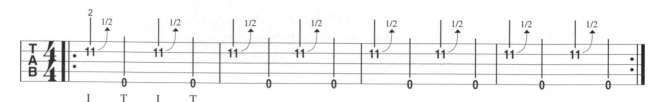

Partial Chord Shapes

Several pieces in this book use *partial chord shapes*. Each shape uses notes from F, D, or A closed-position chord shapes. However, only the notes played are held down with the left hand, hence the name "partial chord shape." It's a good idea to visualize and understand what F, D, or A chord each of the partial chord shapes correspond with. This will help make visible the logic of the fretboard. Knowing *why* you put your fingers down helps you remember *where* you put them.

Partial Chord Tutorial

Here's the key used throughout this book for partial chords:

◯ = unused notes in chord

● = notes held down

The following partial chord shapes are used in "Goin' Down That Road Feelin' Bad."

The G chord uses part of the A barre shape:

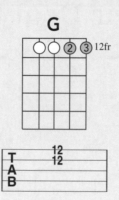

The C and D chords each use part of the F shape:

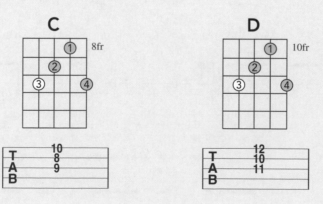

The following high break arrangement of "Goin' Down That Road Feelin' Bad" uses partial chord shapes. It'd be a good idea to play backup along with the track using the full chords in all three chord zones.

Goin' Down That Road Feelin' Bad
(High Break)

▶ Play backup using the full chord shapes and visualize the partial chords within them. The more points of familiarity you perceive, the easier it will be to navigate the neck with confidence.

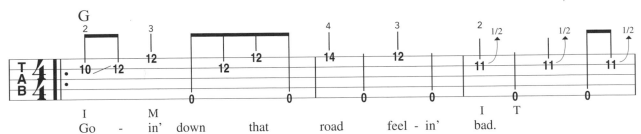

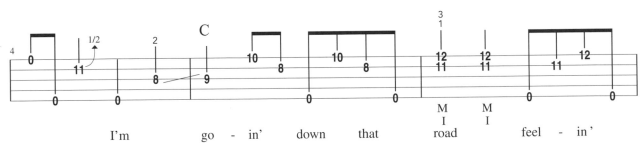

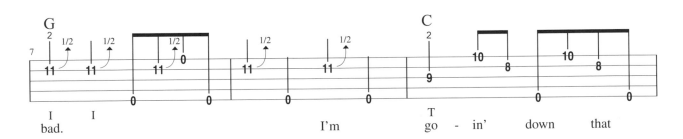

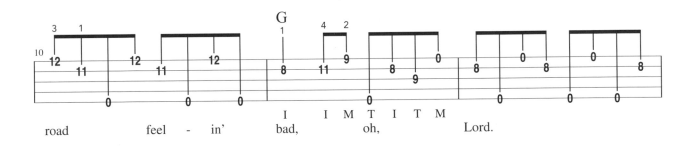

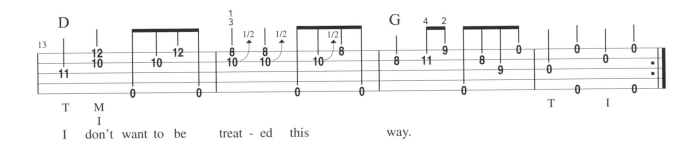

57

Lesson 15 Melodic Style

Track 113

The *melodic style* differs from bluegrass in both execution and sound. As a general rule, every note is played on a different string—some open, some fretted. This results in a smooth, melodious sound from the banjo. The melodic style is much less dependent on right-hand picking patterns than bluegrass. The left hand makes ample use of partial chord shapes and alterations thereof. It's not unusual for every note in a melodic arrangement to be a melody note (another big difference from bluegrass). Banjoist Bill Keith developed this technique as a way of tackling fiddle tunes on the banjo.

The three G scale positions here apply directly to the following tunes: "Turkey in the Straw," "The Flowers of Edinburgh," "The Road to Lisdoonvarna," "Planxty Irwin," "The Kesh Jig," "The Irish Washerwoman," "Blackberry Blossom," and "Mason's Apron."

G Major Scale: Three Ways to Play It

Track 114

▶ Be sure to keep the left-hand fingers on their notes until after you play the next note. This will dovetail the ringing notes into each other for a smooth, flowing sound.

Basic:

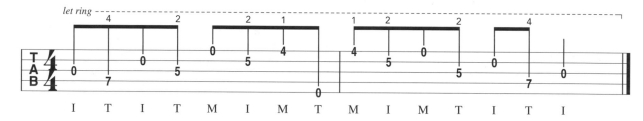

This one involves wrapping the fret-hand thumb around the neck to fret the 5th string.

Track 115

Extended:

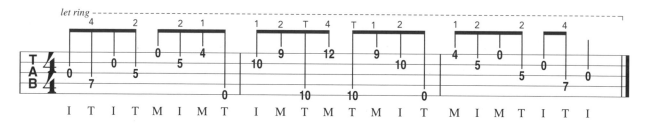

Here's a New Way Up:

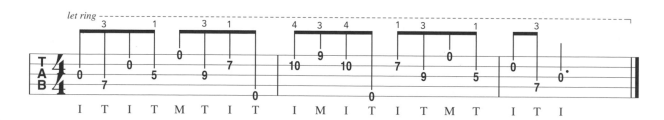

Recommended Listening: Tony Trischka, Bill Keith, and Béla Fleck's *Fiddle Tunes for Banjo* (Rounder #3719).

58

Reels

Let's keep it reel folks. A *reel* is both a tune and a type of folk dance. Common in Scotland and Ireland, the reel is characterized by its rhythm, which accents the first and third beats of each measure. Reels usually have two *sections* (A and B); in most reels, each section is repeated (to create an AABB form). The melody often follows a scheme of a two-measure question and a two-measure answer phrase. Did I mention they sound wonderful on the banjo?

Two New Partial Chords

"Turkey in the Straw" uses two new partial chords to add to your expanding library.

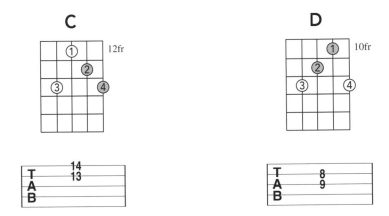

Music History

"Turkey in the Straw" is a well-known American folk song from the early 19th century. It was first popularized in the 1820s and '30s. Though not directly Scotch-Irish in origin, it does fit into the category of reels. It's also a popular ice cream truck melody! What's better than a banjo? A banjo *and* ice cream.

Following the Roadmap

You may notice some new roadmap directions in the next song. *D.S. al Coda* means to go to the sign (𝄋), play to the measure with the *To Coda* sign, then jump directly to the *Coda* section.

Turkey in the Straw

► "Turkey in the Straw" also uses a third partial chord you've already learned; can you find it?

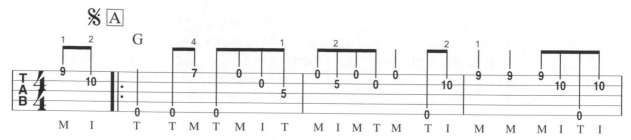

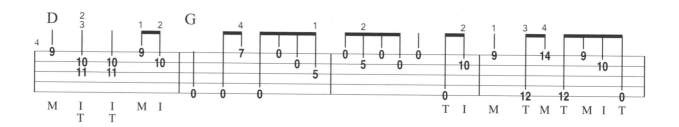

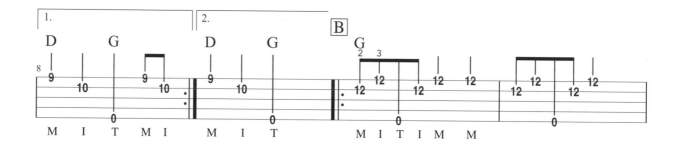

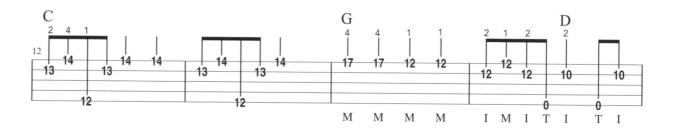

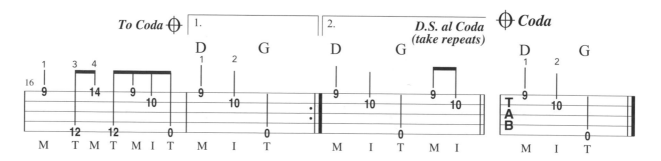

Backing Up

When playing backup, your primary purpose is to support the lead singer or instrument. This means providing a good rhythm and harmonic support by emphasizing chord tones. One must be careful, however, to not interfere with the melody.

Following the Roadmap

A new roadmap direction appears in the next song: **D.C.** This means go to the top of the form and play all the way through the song again.

Turkey in the Straw
(Backup)

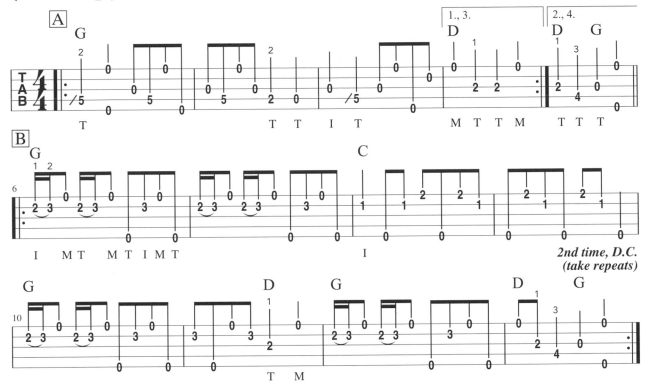

What's a Major Scale?

A *major scale* has seven different notes, with the "eighth" note being an octave higher than the first (as with the G scale you learned). The eight notes are arranged in a pattern of *whole steps* (the distance of two frets) and *half steps* (the distance of one fret). These two distances between notes are called *intervals*. The pattern of intervals for all major scales is W–W–H–W–W–W–H. Here's how that looks on the neck:

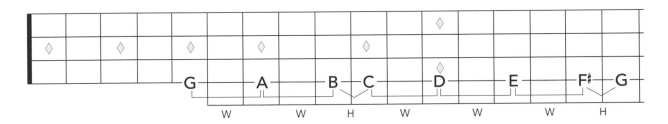

Here's the same thing in tab. Use the first finger of the left hand to play the following notes.

G Major Along One String

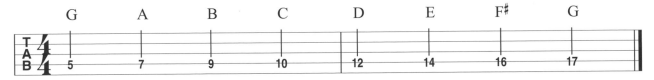

Change One Note

To play a D major scale, we need to change one note from the G scale. The first note of the D major scale is the note D. If you look at the notes of the G scale and read the intervals from D to D, you'll see that they are W–W–H–W–W–H–W. This is not the major scale pattern. We need our pattern back! To do this, we raise the last note by one half step and *poof!*

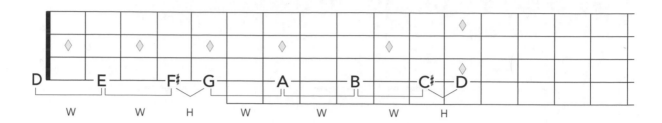

D Major Along One String

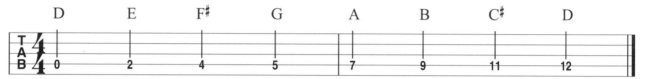

► Look at the letter names of the G and D scales and you'll see that they differ by just one note: C♯.

D Major: Three Ways to Play It

Track 121

Basic:

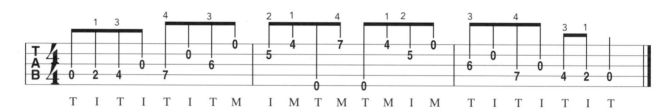

Track 122

Extended:

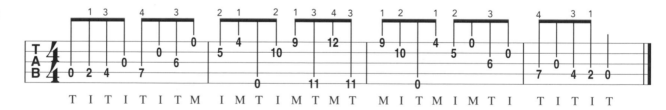

A New Way Up:

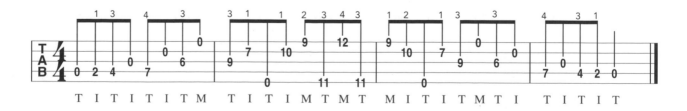

The Silver Spear

Track 123

► Listen for the triplets that are played the second time through the tune, then check out the exercises that follow.

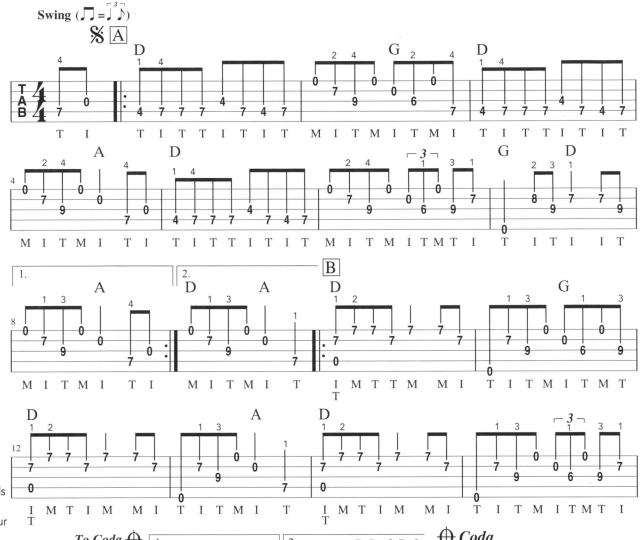

► In the last measure, "Harm." stands for *harmonic*. Simply lay your fingers over the 7th fret wire without pushing down and strum the strings for a chiming effect.

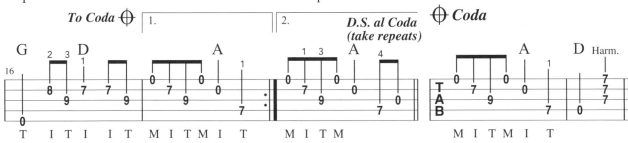

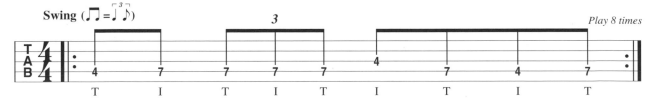

Triplets for the Silver Spear

Track 124

The triplets replicate what you might hear played on the fiddle or bagpipes. The triplets below are played the second time through the tune on the track. They occur in measures 1, 3, and 5. Enjoy 'em!

Track 125

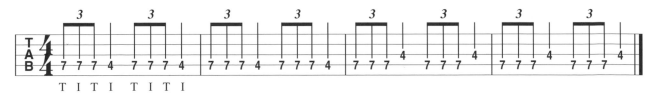

Here's a nice way to get the hang of triplets:

6/8 Time

Track 126

So far everything in this book has been written in a 4/4 *time signature*. The top number of the 4/4 time signature indicates there are four beats in each measure of music. The bottom number indicates that a quarter note gets counted as one beat. (Each quarter note takes up one beat, so four quarter notes equal one measure.) Now let's change the numbers! Our next tune is in **6/8 time**. Each measure now has six beats (6), and each eighth note (8) is worth one beat. Six eighth notes equal one measure of 6/8 time.

Play these notes using the thumb and index fingers of the right hand:

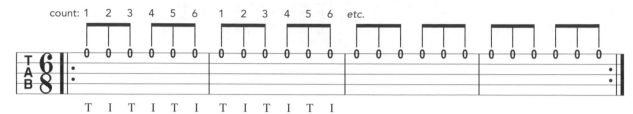

Track 127

In any time signature, a quarter note is always twice as long as an eighth note. Remember that, in 6/8 time, an eighth note gets one beat, so in 6/8 time, quarter notes get counted as two beats. Fancy math indeed!

Track 128

Dotted Quarter Notes

Track 129

When you see a *dot* after a note, you increase its value by 1/2. In 6/8 time, each eighth note gets one beat (remember that is what the bottom number of the time signature tells us), and each quarter note gets two beats. When there is dot after a quarter, we add half its value (one beat), so a dotted quarter receives three beats. Two of them fit into each six-beat measure.

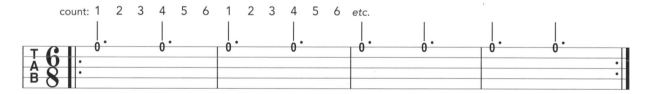

Track 130

Dotted Eighth Notes

Track 131

In 6/8 time, we know each eighth note gets a beat. If we divide an eighth note in half, we have two sixteenth notes. When we dot a note, we increase its value by 1/2, so a dotted eighth is increased in duration by a sixteenth note. The dotted eighth takes up the time of three sixteenth notes. Each dotted eighth in the example below is followed by a sixteenth note, which receives a quick half beat. Be sure to listen to this rhythm on the track to help it make more sense!

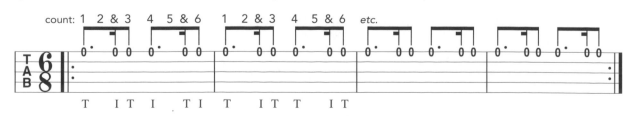

Track 132

Planxty Irwin

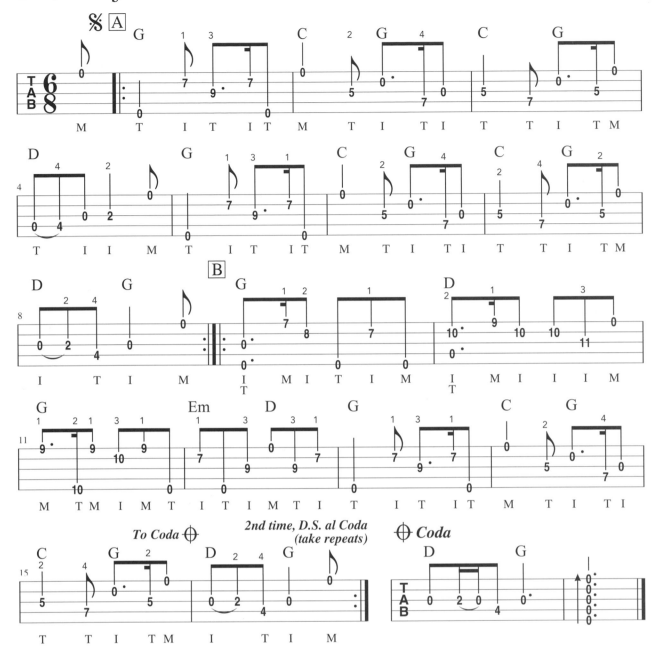

On the recording, you'll hear the last measure of the A and B section sometimes played like this:

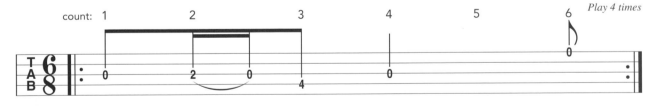

Music History

A *planxty* refers to a piece of music written as a tribute to a person, usually a patron of the composer. Traveling musicians wrote songs for others in return for beds, meals, or bills paid. In return, the patron was honored by their name being used as the title for the composition. "Planxty Irwin" was written by traveling Harper-composer Turlough O'Carolan (1670–1738) for Colonel John Irwin. A plaque in St. Patrick's Cathedral in Dublin honors O'Carolan as "the last of the Irish bards"—the man who brought to a close the centuries-old tradition of the wandering poet minstrel.

Going Modal

Track 135

Modes are an ancient system of organizing musical tones common in medieval liturgical music. There are seven modes, each relating to a note of the major scale. You have already played the first mode: *Ionian* (also known as the "major scale")! The second mode is *Dorian*. You can play the Dorian mode by starting any major scale on its second note. Starting on the second note of the scale changes the order of half and whole steps, and that changes the scale's sound. Our next tune, "The Road to Lisdoonvarna" is in the Dorian mode. In this tune, we start the D major scale on its second note, E. This is called E Dorian.

E Dorian Along One String

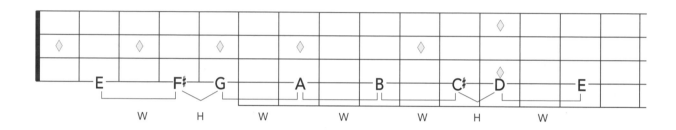

Play the scale below. Prime your ears by strumming E minor (measure 1). If you can make the stretch, use the 2nd finger where indicated to allow the notes to ring as much as possible. These sounds perhaps invoke the cool, foggy woods along the road to Lisdoonvarna.

Track 136

Dipping into Dorian

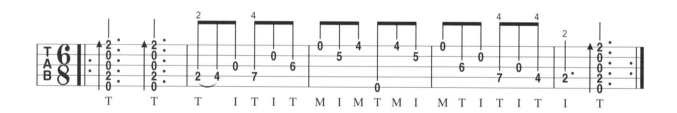

Music History

Plato felt that playing music in a certain mode would incline one towards specific feelings and behaviors associated with that mode. He suggested that soldiers listen to music in the Dorian mode to make them feel stronger. He also believed that a change in the musical modes of the state would cause a wide-scale social revolution.

This is a traditional Irish fiddle tune. Lisdoonvarna is a town in County Clare, Ireland.

Track 137

The Road to Lisdoonvarna

► Whenever you see the note C♯ (a number 6 on the middle line), hold that note down as long as you can!

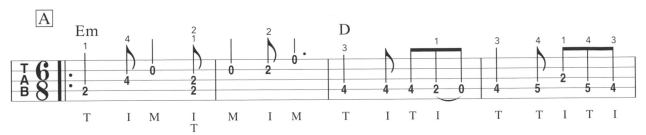

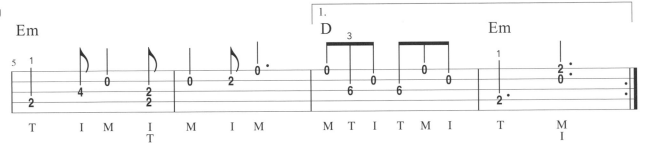

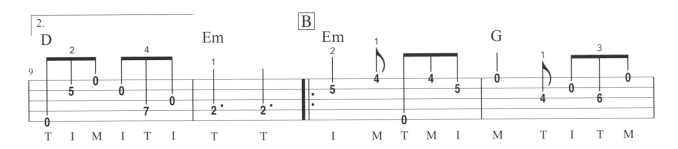

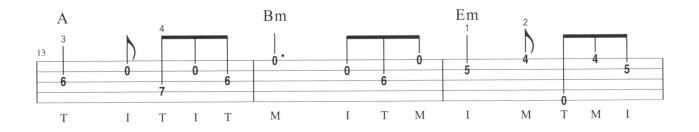

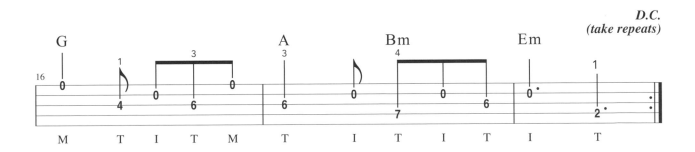

Lesson 19 Jigs

Track 138

The term *jig* refers both to a tune and the accompanying dance. Jigs are in 6/8 time. Before playing these roll patterns, listen to the track. They are played with a rhythmic, "Irish lilt."

Three Rolls in 6/8 Time

The three following roll patterns will warm you up to the jig rhythm.

Track 139

The *forward-reverse roll* works well in 6/8 time:

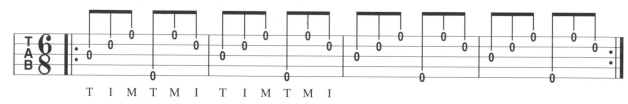

Track 140

Here's a variation:

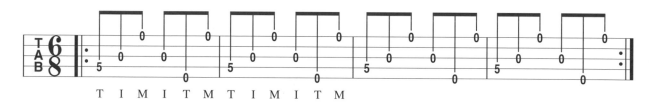

Track 141

One more:

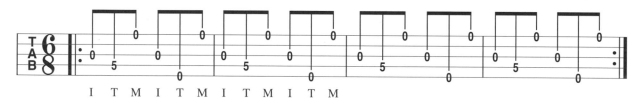

Music History

The term "jig" springs from two possible sources: the French word "Gigue," meaning "small fiddle," or the Italian word "*Giga,*" which refers to a short piece of music popular in the Middle Ages. Irish jigs are short tunes commonly played on the fiddle.

Track 142

In measure 4 of "The Irish Washerwoman," there is a hammer-on of two notes at once. Play the example below to get the hang of it. The strings are not picked before you hammer on the notes. The sound produced has tone, but its primary function is rhythmic. The hammer-on provides a percussive sound to keep the jig rhythm dancing along. The 1st finger can stay down the whole time while the 2nd and 3rd fingers execute the hammer-ons. Be sure to give this a listen on the track.

Track 143

Double Hammer-On

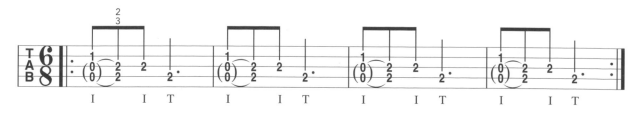

This tune is sometimes sung and played as a song.

Track 144

The Irish Washerwoman

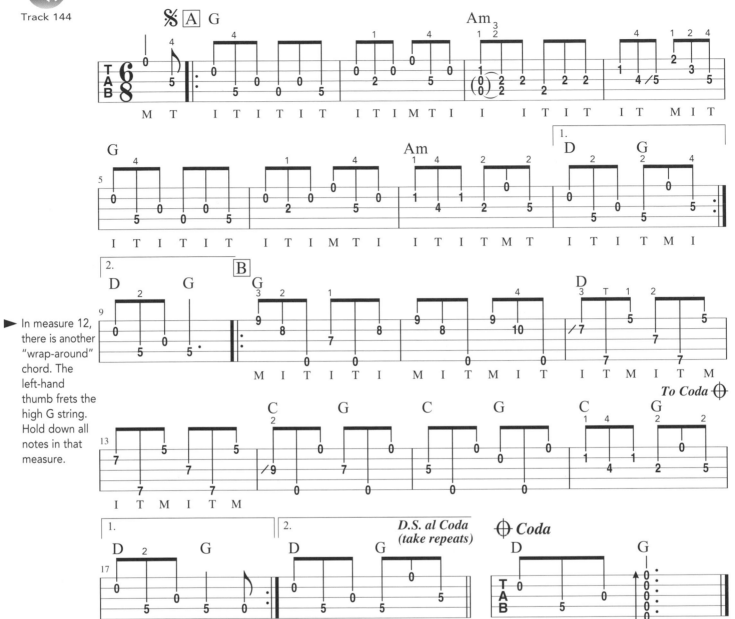

In measure 12, there is another "wrap-around" chord. The left-hand thumb frets the high G string. Hold down all notes in that measure.

Recommended Listening: Irish fiddlers and bagpipers to enjoy and absorb the nuances of Irish music.

New Partial Chords

The B section of this backup arrangement makes use of the following partial chords:

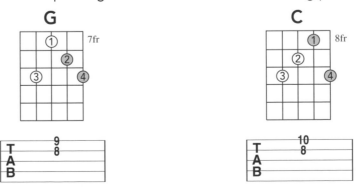

The Irish Washerwoman
(Backup)

Track 145

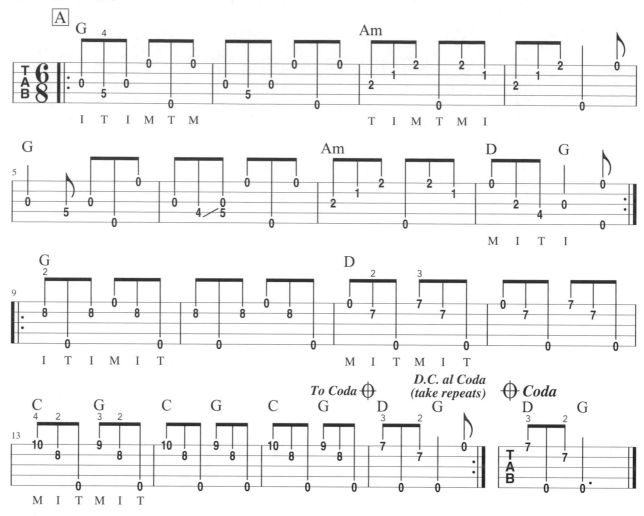

Kesh is a small village in County Fermanagh, Northern Ireland. It is situated on the Kesh River.

The Kesh Jig

Track 146

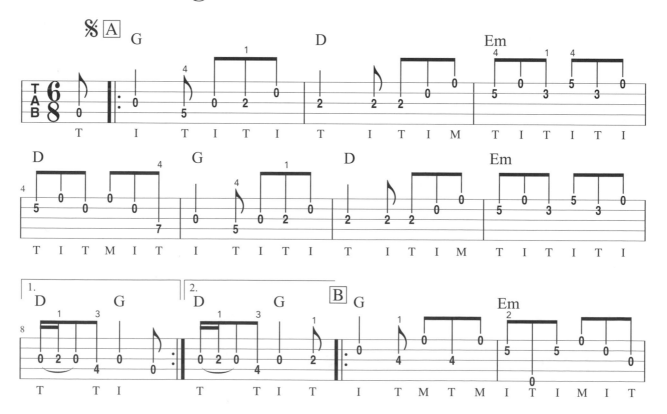

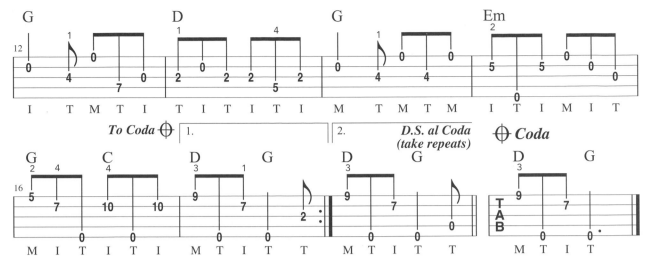

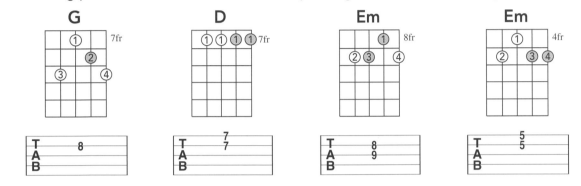

New Partial Chords

The following partial chords are used in the backup arrangement of "The Kesh Jig."

Now enjoy a melodious take on backup for "The Kesh Jig."

The Kesh Jig (Backup)

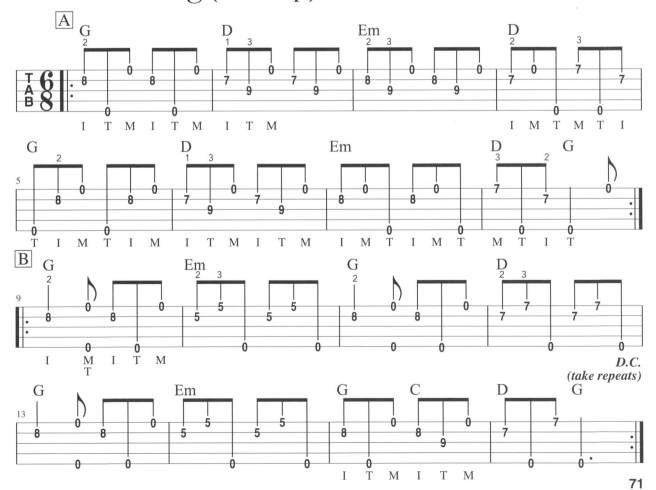

Hornpipes

The *hornpipe* is a tune in 4/4 time similar to the reel. Unlike reels, however, hornpipes are played with a distinct, rhythmic lilt or swing, whereas reels are played "straight." This difference in rhythmic feel is notated with a "swing" icon above the music. Listen to the recording (and to Irish fiddle tunes) to absorb the rhythmic nuances as well.

Music History

The term "hornpipe" refers to both a dance **and** a musical style. One would dance the hornpipe to a hornpipe. Hornpipes have been played and danced since the 17th century. The hornpipe is also the name of an ancient wind instrument made from a cow horn that is sometimes converted into a bagpipe.

This tune is commonly played as a reel or played at light speed by bluegrass musicians. Here the tune is set as an easy-going hornpipe.

Blackberry Blossom

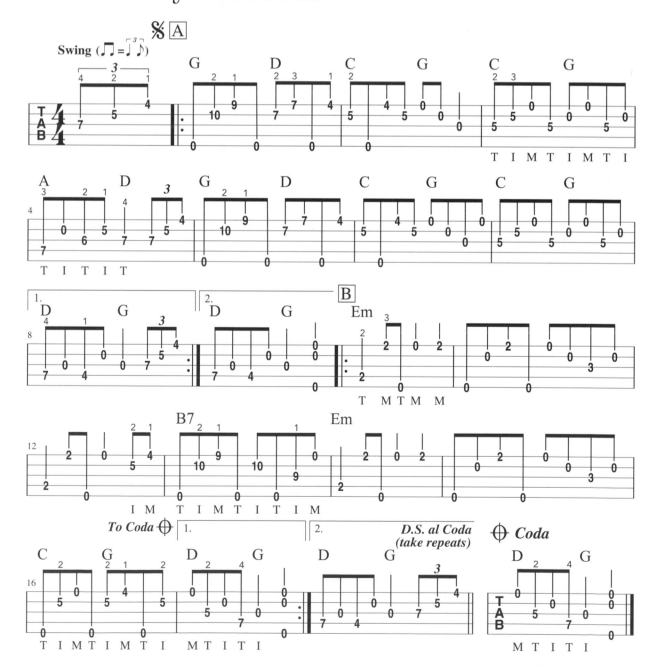

Blackberry Blossom (Backup)

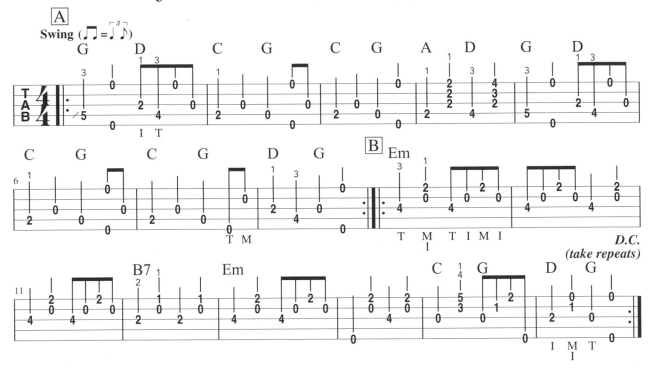

Edinburgh is the capital city of Scotland. Throughout the city are world-renowned parks and gardens.

Flowers of Edinburgh

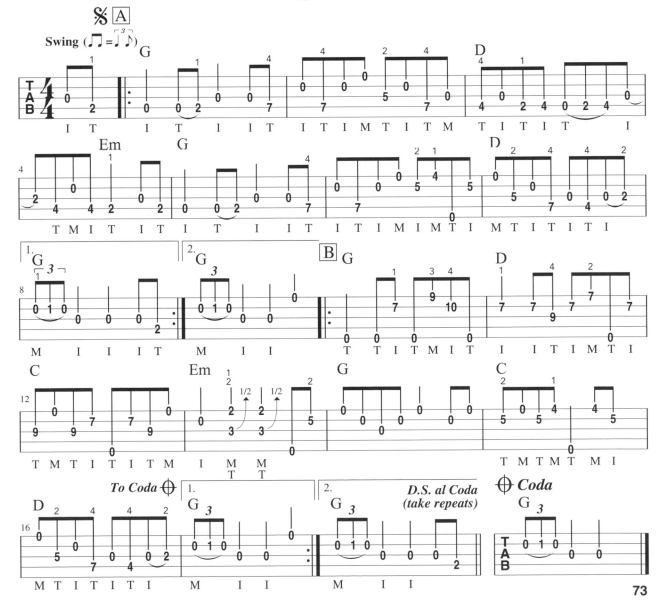

73

Polkas

Track 152

Polkas are almost always written and played in *2/4 time* (two beats per measure).

Music History

The polka is a lively Central European dance and a genre of dance music familiar throughout Europe and the Americas. It originated in the mid-19th century in Bohemia and is still a common genre in Czech, German, Austrian, Slovakian, and Polish folk music. In Milwaukee, Wisconsin, the polka's still keepin' time!

The Irish band, Planxty, recorded this tune in 1979. They called it "John Ryan's Polka."

Sean Ryan's Polka

Track 153

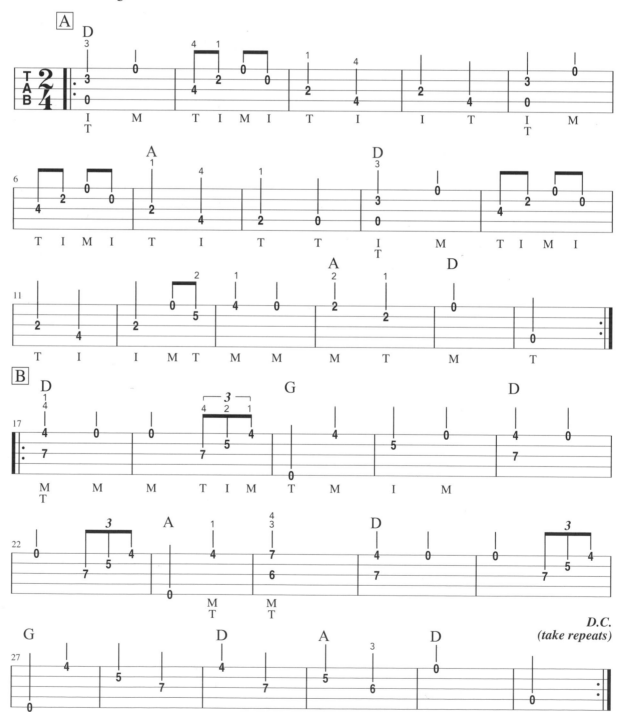

D.C.
(take repeats)

74

Sean Ryan's Polka
(High Break)

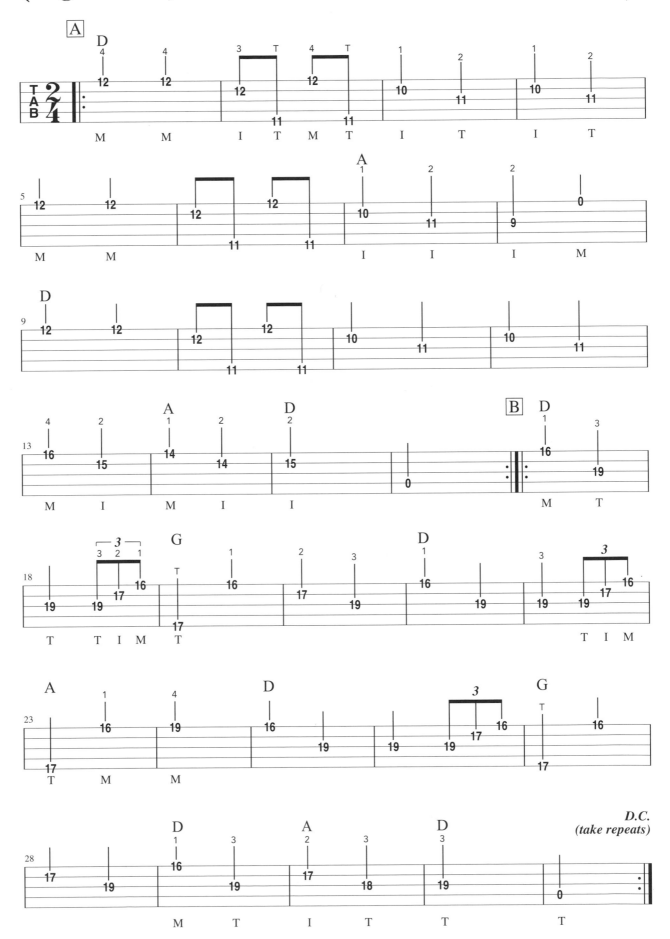

D.C.
(take repeats)

75

Single-String Style

Track 155

Single-string style is where you play several notes in a row on the same string. The predominant right-hand fingering is T–I–T–I. This style first came to widespread attention thanks t o Don Reno. Béla Fleck incorporates the single-string style into his playing. Because there is usually only one note sounding at a time, the single-string style produces a punchy sound all its own.

Single-String Exercises

Play with a relaxed, even sound.

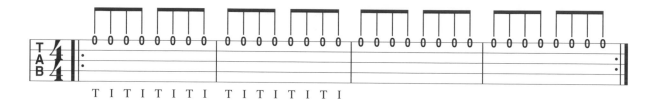

Track 156

Play across four strings.

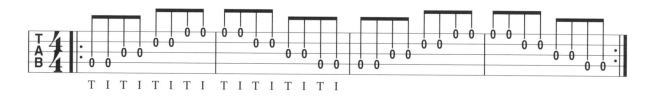

Track 157

From low to high…

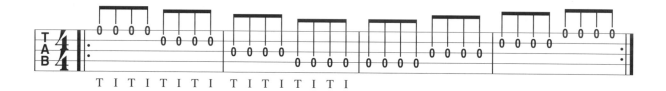

Track 158

Leaving spaces…

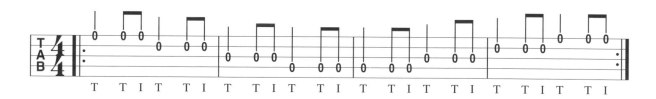

Track 159

Crossing under...

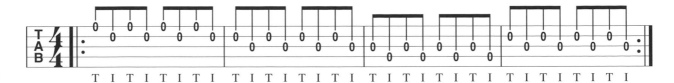

Track 160

Name this tune!

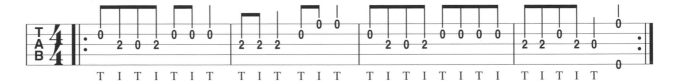

Track 161

> **Recommended Listening**: Don Reno and Béla Fleck. For a wide range of musical ideas that may work well with the single-string technique, listen to other instrumentalists (horn players, guitar players, etc.).

Track 162

Single-String Scales

The logic and linear nature of the single-string style makes it a wonderful way to visualize and learn scales. The G major scales below are both related to the F-shape G chord at fret 5.

Track 163

G Major #1

This scale plays straight through the F-shape G chord.

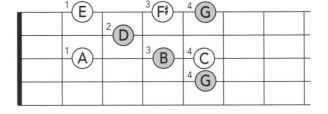

Here it is in tab.

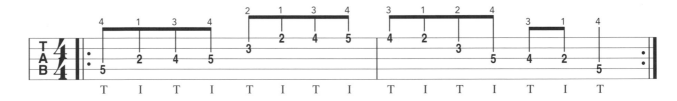

G Major #2

This G scale plays in front of the F-shape G chord.

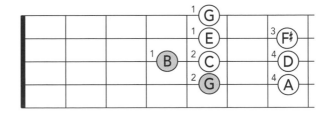

Here it is in tab.

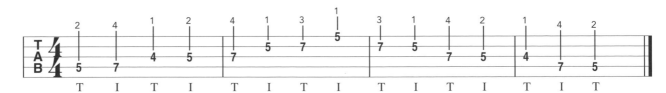

77

These are movable scales! Try them two frets higher and you're playing in A major. Here's one position that plays through the F shape in the key of A.

Track 164

A Major

► Find the one played in front of the F shape on your own.

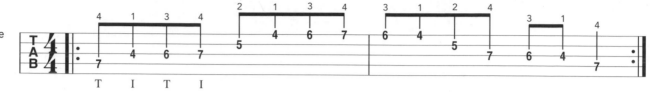

Track 165

Mixolydian Mode

A simple way to find the Mixolydian mode is to play any major scale and lower the seventh note scale by one half step (one fret).

A Mixolydian

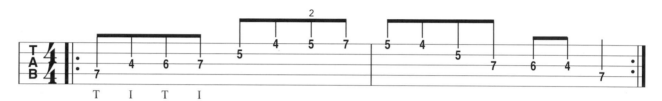

Here's another A Mixolydian scale.

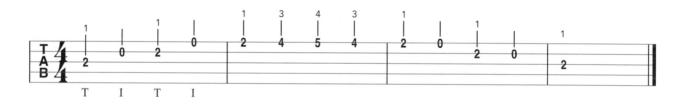

Modal Tip

You can also describe the Mixolydian mode as any major scale starting on its fifth note. If you play a D scale (D–E–F♯–G–A–B–C♯) starting on its fifth note, A, you're playing A Mixolydian (A–B–C♯–D–E–F♯–G). How elegant.

"Red Haired Boy" belongs to the reel family of tunes. It's also sometimes called "The Little Beggar Man." It is in the Mixolydian mode, and it's a real tune, indeed.

Red Haired Boy

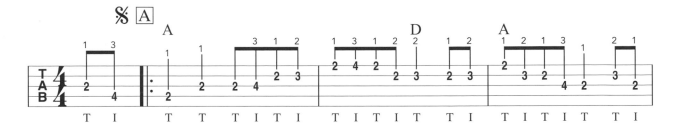

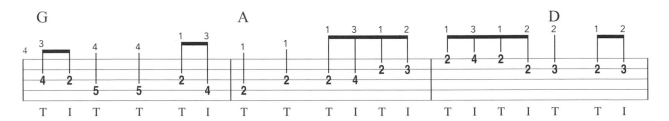

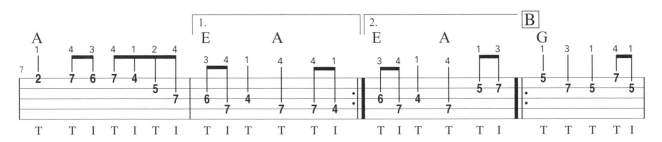

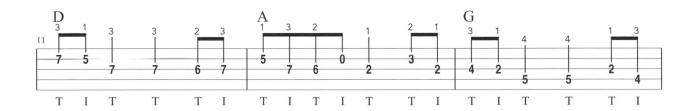

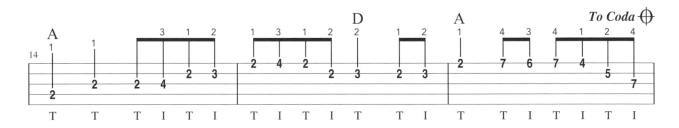

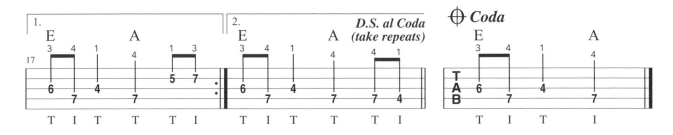

Harmony

Track 167

Many books have been written on this subject. Webster's Dictionary offers a simple definition: "A musical agreement of sounds." The banjo is commonly tuned to a G chord. When you strum all of the strings, they are ringing in harmony with each other. A melody can be harmonized by playing along with different notes from the song's scale. This is what background singers often do. It is common to play a harmony part by starting on the note that is three scale steps higher from each melody note. Doing this is called "harmonizing in 3rds." Each harmony note is either a **major 3rd** (two whole steps above the melody note) or a **minor 3rd** (1 1/2 steps up).

After you learn this, play along with the track. You are now harmonizing!

Track 168

Red Haired Boy
(Melody Played up a 3rd)

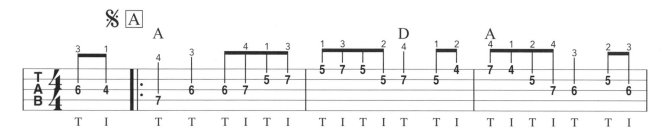

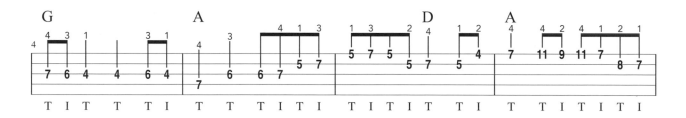

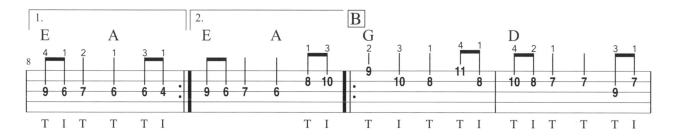

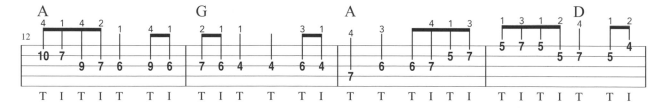

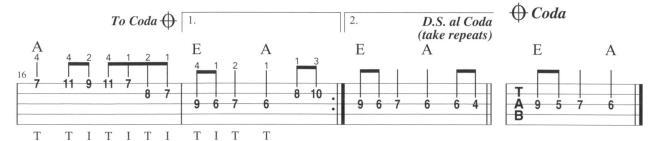

More Single-String Scales

The D scale below is associated with the D chord shape. These are all scale tones; the D shape is shaded for you to see. Play it ascending and descending.

Here it is in tab:

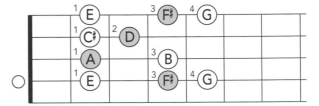

This next scale lies in front of the D shape. Visualize it as playing up to the A (or barre) shape D chord at the 7th fret (shaded area). This starts on the third note of the D scale (F♯), but now you play that note with the first finger of your left hand.

Here it is in tab:

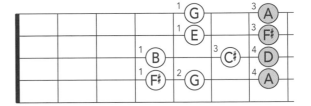

The Silver Spear High Break Ideas

After familiarizing yourself with D scales (and their associated chord shapes), play them up an octave. Start by finding the D-shape D chord above the 12th fret. Play the scale through the chord just as you did in the lower position, then play the second scale up to the next D chord, the A shape, at the 19th fret. This is the region where lies our next tune, "The Silver Spear."

The triplets played in "The Silver Spear" are treated as ornaments. They in themselves are not integral to the melody of the tune—they're icing on the cake. When used tastefully, ornaments provide variation. If they were used all the time in the same way, they would fail to provide contrast.

Some Ornament Alternatives

Repeat the excerpts below as written to get a fluent, easy feel so they can be used at your will and whimsy.

The first measure below works well in measures 1, 3, and 5.

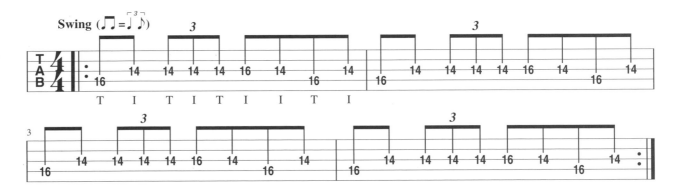

The triplet in measure 6 crosses strings. Here it is isolated for practice.

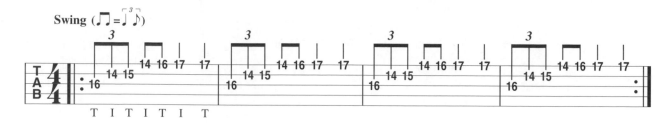

Here's the same measure with no triplets.

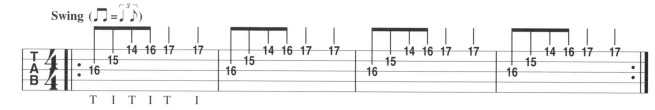

T–I–M Triplets

The following method allows you to play rapid-fire triplets with minimal effort. They are picked with the thumb, index, and middle fingers of the right hand (T–I–M).

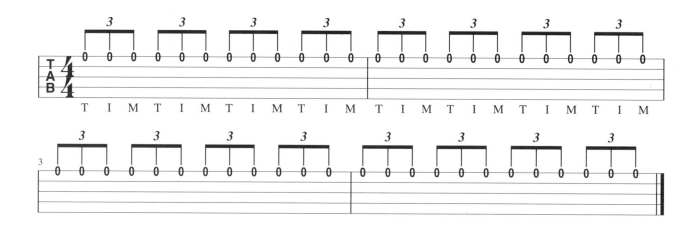

The triplets below fit well in measures 12 and 14.

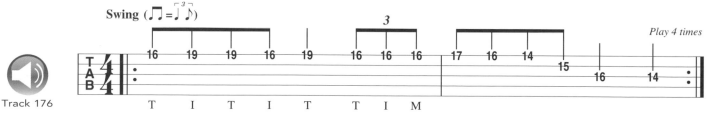

The Silver Spear
(Single-String High Break)

Track 177

► Perhaps it'd be fun for you to explore playing this high break an octave lower.

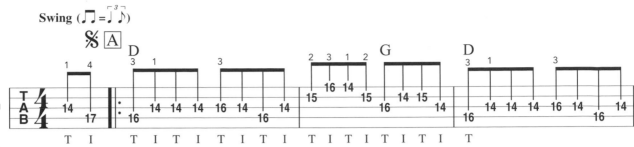

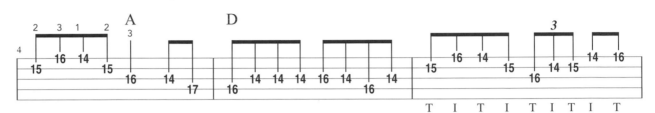

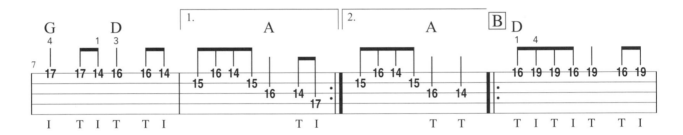

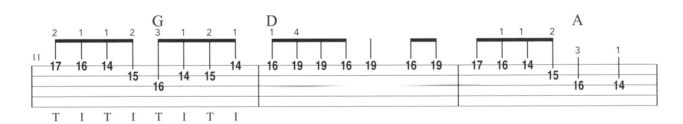

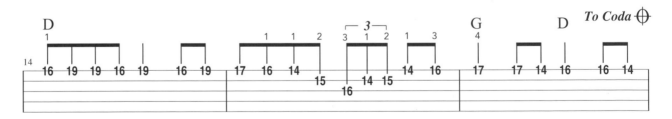

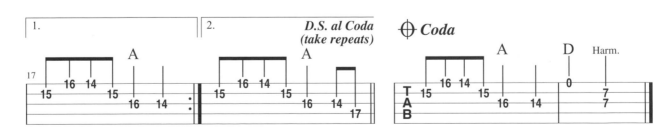

83

Single-String Style in 6/8

Switching Fingers

When playing single-string triplets, you'll notice that the first group of three notes starts with the right-hand thumb, while the second group starts with the index finger.

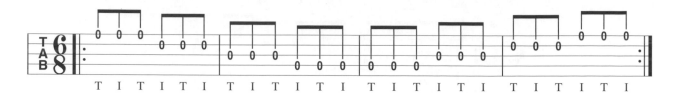

D Major Scale—Open Position

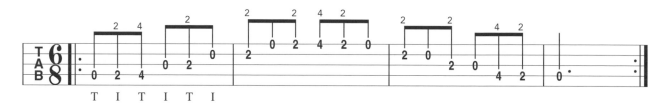

D Mixolydian

We can play D Mixolydian by flatting the seventh note of the D major scale.

► D Mixolydian is the same as starting the G major scale on its fifth note, D.

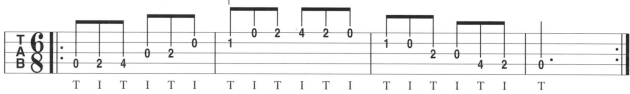

"Banish Misfortune?" Sounds like a good idea. Learning this three-part jig in D Mixolydian is surely a good start.

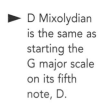

Banish Misfortune

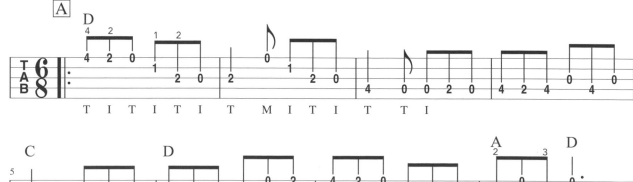

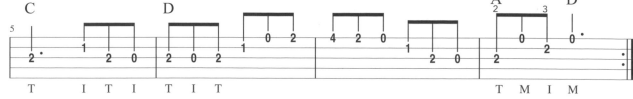

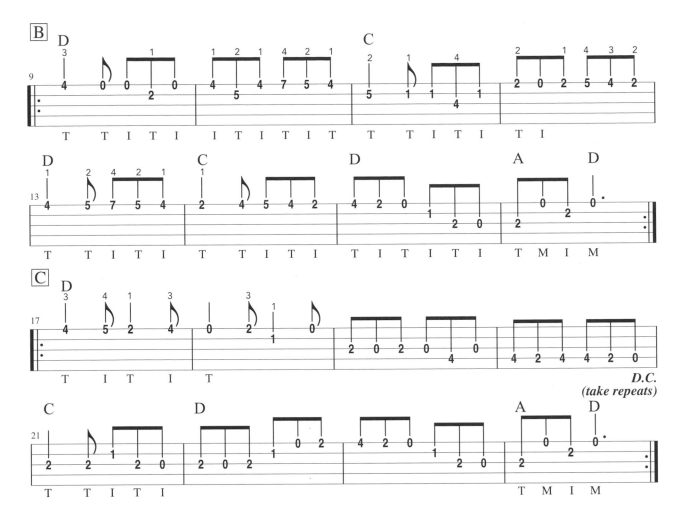

Banish Misfortune Ornament Alternatives

Track 182

When you play notes in a series of half steps (no fret in between), it is called **chromatic**.

Measures 8 and 16 are nice places for this little chromatic run.

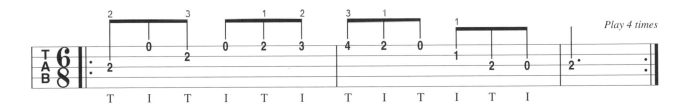

Play 4 times

Here's a hammer-on/pull-off ornament that sounds nice in measure 15.

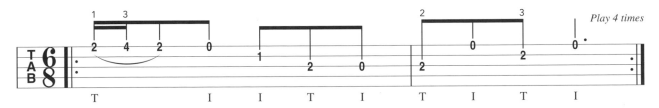

Play 4 times

Track 183

Here's another place for an ornament in measure 17.

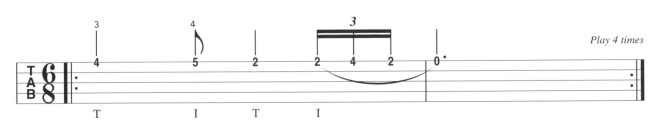

Play 4 times

Track 184

85

The Road to Lisdoonvarna
(High Break)

► The pull-off in measure 3 could also be picked with the index finger instead.

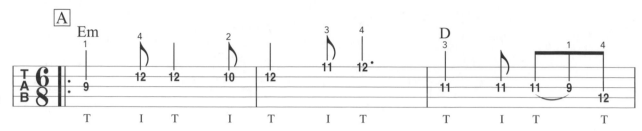

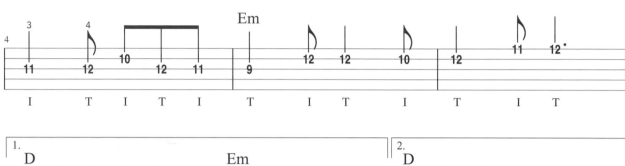

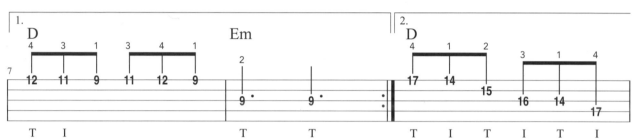

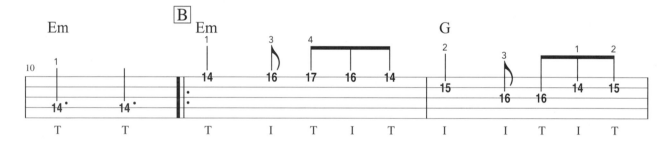

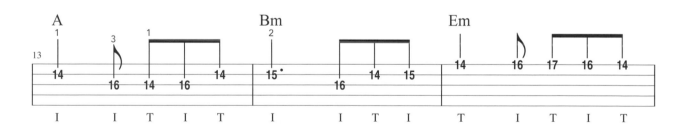

D.C.
(take repeats)

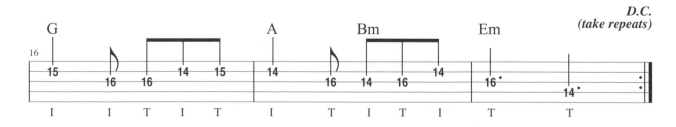

Combining Styles

Track 186

Track 187

The contrasting sound of the single-string and melodic styles can work together in the same piece. Here are four pieces that use both styles.

Red Haired Boy

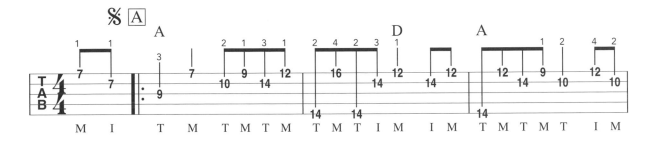

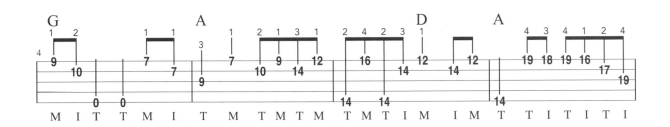

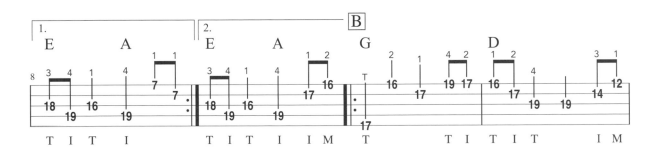

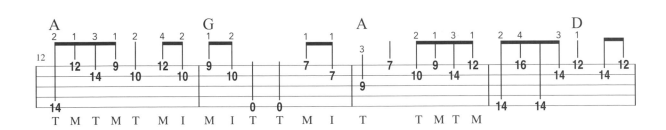

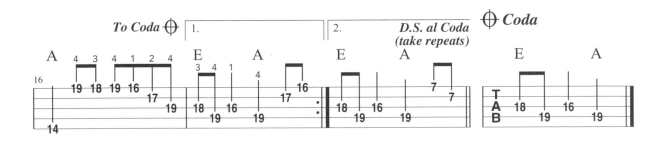

The Mason's Apron

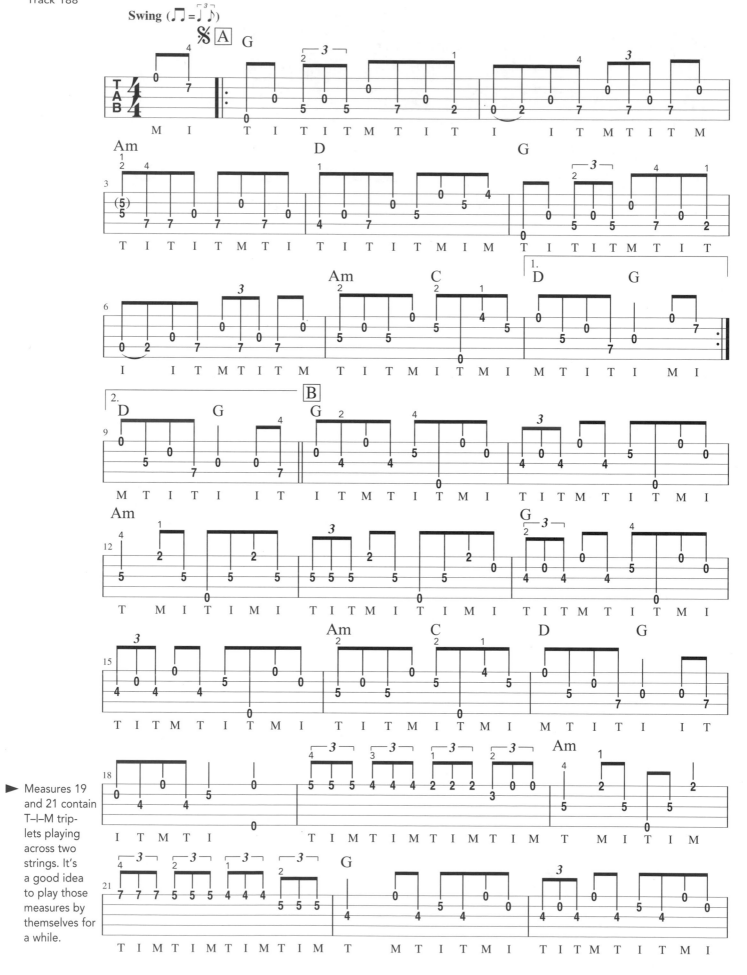

Measures 19 and 21 contain T–I–M triplets playing across two strings. It's a good idea to play those measures by themselves for a while.

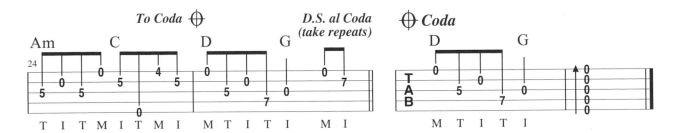

Fisher's Hornpipe

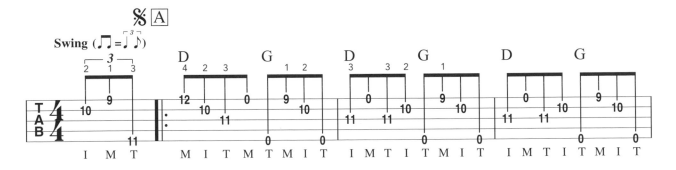

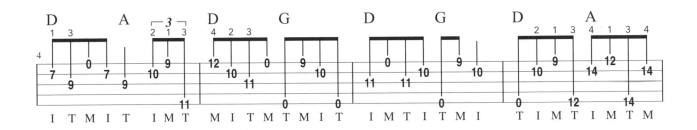

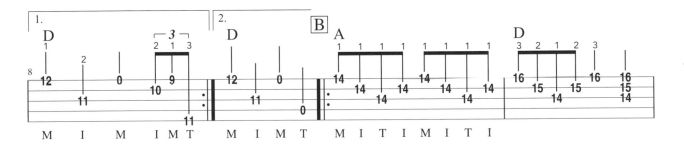

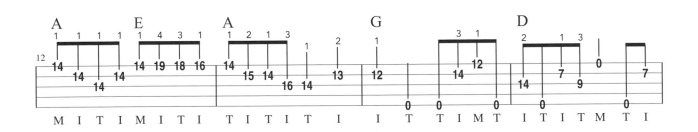

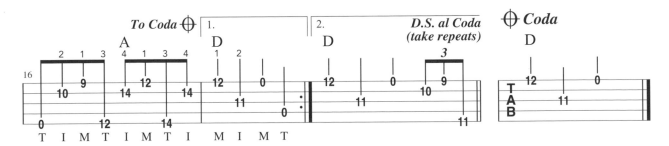

Morrison's Jig

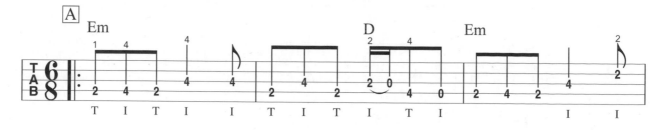

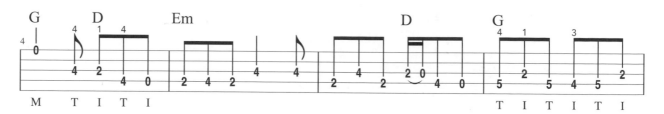

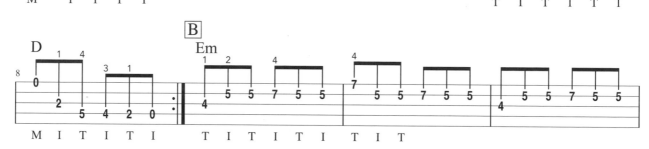

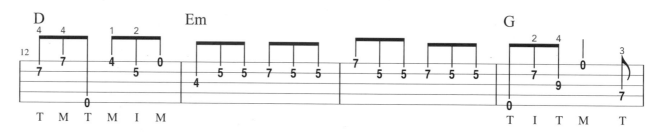

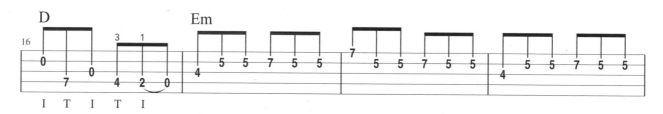

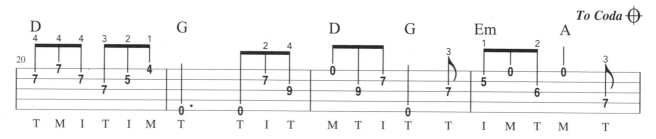

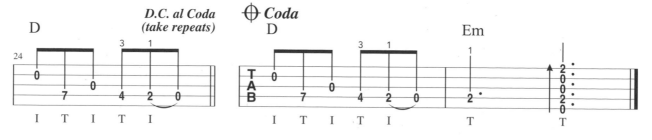

Lesson 24 | Chord Melody

Track 191

Many pieces in this book (and just about everywhere else) have melodies and chords. In music it's common to have someone play the chords (backup) while another player takes the melody or solo. In a chord melody arrangement, however, you play both the chords and the melody at the same time! Much has been written about chord melody for jazz guitar. The art of playing and arranging in this style has much to do with selecting a chord that sounds right with the melody while selecting notes from the chord that both imply its quality (major, minor, etc.) and support the melody. Common notes used are the root, 3rd, 5th, 6th, and 7th notes of the given chord. Conveniently, you need not (and could not) play the entire chord—just your well-selected notes from it. The chord melody approach gives the music a full sound and enables the banjoist to play unaccompanied. An entire book could be written on this subject!

Track 192

Auld Lang Syne

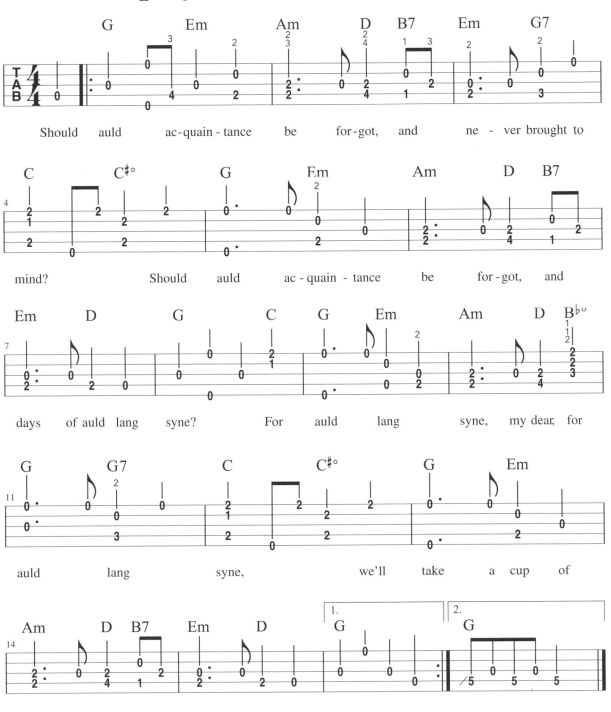

America the Beautiful

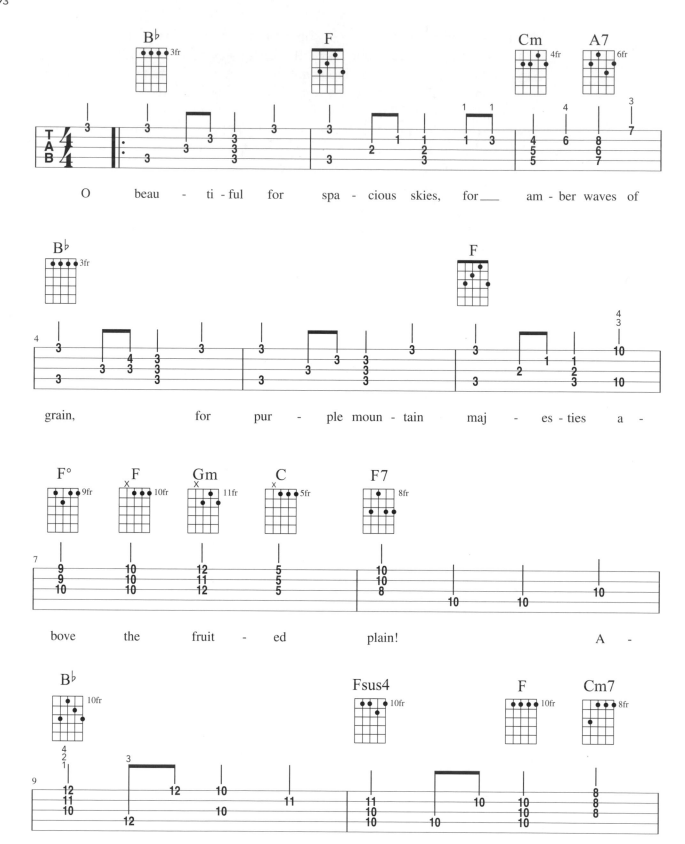

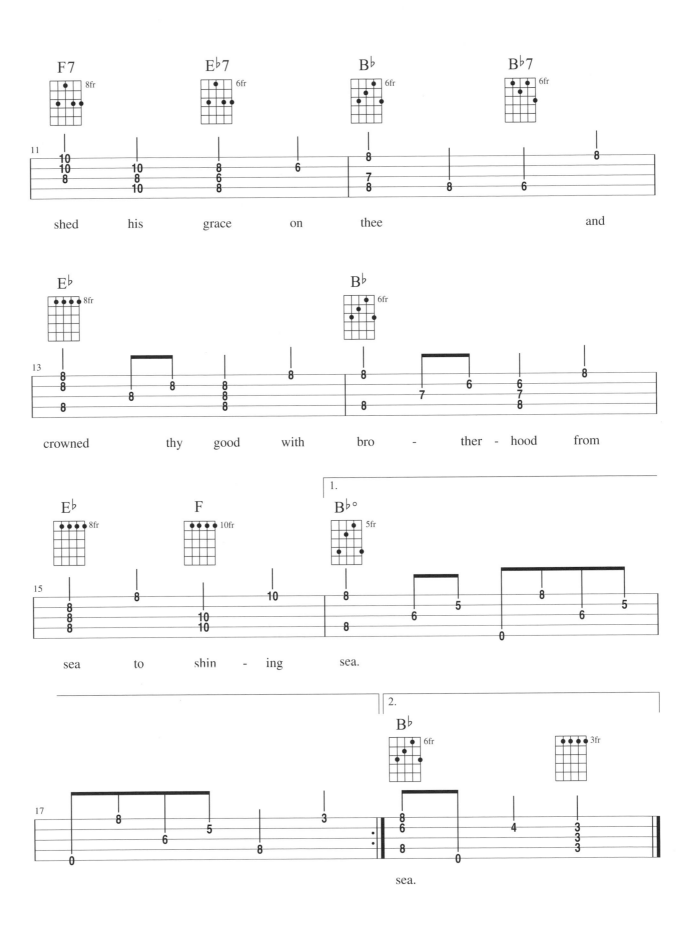

Play Today! Series

The Ultimate Self-Teaching Series

These are complete guides to the basics, designed to offer quality instruction, terrific songs, and professional-quality audio with tons of full-demo tracks and instruction. Each book includes over 70 great songs and examples!

Play Accordion Today!
00701744	Level 1 Book/Audio	$10.99
00702657	Level 1 Songbook Book/Audio	$12.99

Play Alto Sax Today!
00842049	Level 1 Book/Audio	$9.99
00842050	Level 2 Book/Audio	$9.99
00320359	DVD	$14.95
00842051	Songbook Book/Audio	$12.95
00699555	Beginner's – Level 1 Book/Audio & DVD	$19.95
00699492	Play Today Plus Book/Audio	$14.95

Play Banjo Today!
00699897	Level 1 Book/Audio	$9.99
00701006	Level 2 Book/Audio	$9.99
00320913	DVD	$14.99
00115999	Songbook Book/Audio	$12.99
00701873	Beginner's – Level 1 Book/Audio & DVD	$19.95

Play Bass Today!
00842020	Level 1 Book/Audio	$9.99
00842036	Level 2 Book/Audio	$9.99
00320356	DVD	$14.95
00842037	Songbook Book/Audio	$12.95
00699552	Beginner's – Level 1 Book/Audio & DVD	$19.99

Play Cello Today!
00151353	Level 1 Book/Audio	$9.99

Play Clarinet Today!
00842046	Level 1 Book/Audio	$9.99
00842047	Level 2 Book/Audio	$9.99
00320358	DVD	$14.95
00842048	Songbook Book/Audio	$12.95
00699554	Beginner's – Level 1 Book/Audio & DVD	$19.95
00699490	Play Today Plus Book/Audio	$14.95

Play Dobro Today!
00701505	Level 1 Book/Audio	$9.99

Play Drums Today!
00842021	Level 1 Book/Audio	$9.99
00842038	Level 2 Book/Audio	$9.95
00320355	DVD	$14.95
00842039	Songbook Book/Audio	$12.95
00699551	Beginner's – Level 1 Book/Audio & DVD	$19.95
00703291	Starter	$24.99

Play Flute Today
00842043	Level 1 Book/Audio	$9.95
00842044	Level 2 Book/Audio	$9.99
00320360	DVD	$14.95
00842045	Songbook Book/Audio	$12.95
00699553	Beginner's – Level 1 Book/Audio & DVD	$19.95

Play Guitar Today!
00696100	Level 1 Book/Audio	$9.99
00696101	Level 2 Book/Audio	$9.99
00320353	DVD	$14.95
00696102	Songbook Book/Audio	$12.99
00699544	Beginner's – Level 1 Book/Audio & DVD	$19.95
00702431	Worship Songbook Book/Audio	$12.99
00695662	Complete Kit	$29.95

Play Harmonica Today!
00700179	Level 1 Book/Audio	$9.99
00320653	DVD	$14.99
00701875	Beginner's – Level 1 Book/Audio & DVD	$19.95

Play Mandolin Today!
00699911	Level 1 Book/Audio	$9.99
00320909	DVD	$14.99
00115029	Songbook Book/Audio	$12.99
00701874	Beginner's – Level 1 Book/Audio & DVD	$19.99

Play Piano Today! Revised Edition
00842019	Level 1 Book/Audio	$9.99
00298773	Level 2 Book/Audio	$9.95
00842041	Songbook Book/Audio	$12.95
00699545	Beginner's – Level 1 Book/Audio & DVD	$19.95
00702415	Worship Songbook Book/Audio	$12.99
00703707	Complete Kit	$22.99

Play Recorder Today!
00700919	Level 1 Book/Audio	$7.99
00119830	Complete Kit	$19.99

Sing Today!
00699761	Level 1 Book/Audio	$10.99

Play Trombone Today!
00699917	Level 1 Book/Audio	$12.99
00320508	DVD	$14.95

Play Trumpet Today!
00842052	Level 1 Book/Audio	$9.99
00842053	Level 2 Book/Audio	$9.95
00320357	DVD	$14.95
00842054	Songbook Book/Audio	$12.95
00699556	Beginner's – Level 1 Book/Audio & DVD	$19.95

Play Ukulele Today!
00699638	Level 1 Book/Audio	$10.99
00699655	Play Today Plus Book/Audio	$9.99
00320985	DVD	$14.99
00701872	Beginner's – Level 1 Book/Audio & DVD	$19.95
00650743	Book/Audio/DVD with Ukulele	$39.99
00701002	Level 2 Book/Audio	$9.99
00702484	Level 2 Songbook Book/Audio	$12.99
00703290	Starter	$24.99

Play Viola Today!
00142679	Level 1 Book/Audio	$9.99

Play Violin Today!
00699748	Level 1 Book/Audio	$9.99
00701320	Level 2 Book/Audio	$9.99
00321076	DVD	$14.99
00701700	Songbook Book/Audio	$12.99
00701876	Beginner's – Level 1 Book/Audio & DVD	$19.95

HAL•LEONARD®

www.halleonard.com

Hal Leonard Banjo Play-Along Series

HAL·LEONARD® BANJO PLAY-ALONG

AUDIO ACCESS INCLUDED

INCLUDES TAB

*The Banjo Play-Along Series will help you play your favorite songs quickly and easily with incredible backing tracks to help you sound like a bona fide pro! Just follow the banjo tab, listen to the demo track on the CD or online audio to hear how the banjo should sound, and then play along with the separate backing tracks. The CD is playable on any CD player and also is enhanced so Mac and PC users can adjust the recording to any tempo without changing the pitch! Books with online audio also include **PLAYBACK+** options such as looping and tempo adjustments. Each Banjo Play-Along pack features eight cream of the crop songs.*

1. BLUEGRASS
Ashland Breakdown • Deputy Dalton • Dixie Breakdown • Hickory Hollow • I Wish You Knew • I Wonder Where You Are Tonight • Love and Wealth • Salt Creek.
00102585 Book/CD Pack.........................$14.99

2. COUNTRY
East Bound and Down • Flowers on the Wall • Gentle on My Mind • Highway 40 Blues • If You've Got the Money (I've Got the Time) • Just Because • Take It Easy • You Are My Sunshine.
00105278 Book/CD Pack.........................$14.99

3. FOLK/ROCK HITS
Ain't It Enough • The Cave • Forget the Flowers • Ho Hey • Little Lion Man • Live and Die • Switzerland • Wagon Wheel.
00119867 Book/CD Pack.........................$14.99

4. OLD-TIME CHRISTMAS
Away in a Manger • Hark! the Herald Angels Sing • Jingle Bells • Joy to the World • O Holy Night • O Little Town of Bethlehem • Silent Night • We Wish You a Merry Christmas.
00119889 Book/CD Pack.........................$14.99

5. PETE SEEGER
Blue Skies • Get up and Go • If I Had a Hammer (The Hammer Song) • Kisses Sweeter Than Wine • Mbube (Wimoweh) • Sailing Down My Golden River • Turn! Turn! Turn! (To Everything There Is a Season) • We Shall Overcome.
00129699 Book/CD Pack.........................$17.99

6. SONGS FOR BEGINNERS
Bill Cheatham • Black Mountain Rag • Cripple Creek • Grandfather's Clock • John Hardy • Nine Pound Hammer • Old Joe Clark • Will the Circle Be Unbroken.
00139751 Book/CD Pack.........................$14.99

7. BLUEGRASS GOSPEL
Cryin' Holy unto the Lord • How Great Thou Art • I Saw the Light • I'll Fly Away • I'll Have a New Life • Man in the Middle • Turn Your Radio On • Wicked Path of Sin.
00147594 Book/Online Audio $14.99

8. CELTIC BLUEGRASS
Billy in the Low Ground • Cluck Old Hen • Devil's Dream • Fisher's Hornpipe • Little Maggie • Over the Waterfall • The Red Haired Boy • Soldier's Joy.
00160077 Book/Online Audio $14.99

www.halleonard.com

GREAT BANJO PUBLICATIONS
FROM HAL LEONARD

Hal Leonard Banjo Method – Second Edition
by Mac Robertson, Robbie Clement, Will Schmid
This innovative method teaches 5-string banjo bluegrass style using a carefully paced approach that keeps beginners playing great songs *while learning*. Book 1 covers easy chord strums, tablature, right-hand rolls, hammer-ons, slides and pull-offs, and more. Book 2 includes solos and licks, fiddle tunes, back-up, capo use, and more.
00699500 Book 1 Book Only $7.99
00695101 Book 1 Book/Online Audio $16.99
00699502 Book 2 Book Only $7.99

Banjo Aerobics
A 50-Week Workout Program for Developing, Improving and Maintaining Banjo Technique
by Michael Bremer
Take your banjo playing to the next level with this fantastic daily resource, providing a year's worth of practice material with a two-week vacation. The accompanying audio includes demo tracks for all the examples in the book to reinforce how the banjo should sound.
00113734 Book/Online Audio $19.99

Banjo Chord Finder
This extensive reference guide covers over 2,800 banjo chords, including four of the most commonly used tunings. Thirty different chord qualities are covered for each key, and each chord quality is presented in two different voicings. Also includes a lesson on chord construction and a fingerboard chart of the banjo neck!
00695741 9 x 12.................. $8.99 00695742 6 x 9..................... $6.99

Banjo Scale Finder
by Chad Johnson
Learn to play scales on the banjo with this comprehensive yet easy-to-use book. It contains more than 1,300 scale diagrams for the most often-used scales and modes, including multiple patterns for each scale. Also includes a lesson on scale construction and a fingerboard chart of the banjo neck.
00695780 9 x 12.................. $9.99 00695783 6 x 9..................... $6.99

First 50 Songs You Should Play on Banjo
arr. Michael J. Miles & Greg Cahill
Easy-to-read banjo tab, chord symbols and lyrics for the most popular songs banjo players like to play. Explore clawhammer and three-finger-style banjo in a variety of tunings and capoings with this one-of-a-kind collection. Songs include: Angel from Montgomery • Carolina in My Mind • Cripple Creek • Danny Boy • The House of the Rising Sun • Mr. Tambourine Man • Take Me Home, Country Roads • This Land Is Your Land • Wildwood Flower • and many more.
00153311 ....$14.99

Fretboard Roadmaps
by Fred Sokolow
This handy book/with online audio will get you playing all over the banjo fretboard in any key! You'll learn to: increase your chord, scale and lick vocabulary • play chord-based licks, moveable major and blues scales, melodic scales and first-position major scales • and much more! The audio includes 51 demonstrations of the exercises.
00695358 Book/Online Audio $15.99

O Brother, Where Art Thou?
Banjo tab arrangements of 12 bluegrass/folk songs from this Grammy-winning album. Includes: The Big Rock Candy Mountain • Down to the River to Pray • I Am a Man of Constant Sorrow • I Am Weary (Let Me Rest) • I'll Fly Away • In the Jailhouse Now • Keep on the Sunny Side • You Are My Sunshine • and more, plus lyrics and a banjo notation legend.
00699528 Banjo Tablature.. $14.99

Earl Scruggs and the 5-String Banjo
Earl Scruggs' legendary method has helped thousands of banjo players get their start. It features everything you need to know to start playing, even how to build your own banjo! Topics covered include: Scruggs tuners • how to read music • chords • how to read tablature • anatomy of Scruggs-style picking • exercises in picking • 44 songs • biographical notes • and more! The online audio features Earl Scruggs playing and explaining over 60 examples!
00695764 Book Only.. $24.99
00695765 Book/Online Audio... $34.99

Clawhammer Cookbook
Tools, Techniques & Recipes for Playing Clawhammer Banjo
by Michael Bremer
The goal of this book isn't to tell you how to play tunes or how to play like anyone else. It's to teach you ways to approach, arrange, and personalize any tune – to develop your own unique style. To that end, we'll take in a healthy serving of old-time music and also expand the clawhammer palate to taste a few other musical styles. Includes audio track demos of all the songs and examples to aid in the learning process.
00118354 Book/Online Audio...$19.99

The Ultimate Banjo Songbook
A great collection of banjo classics: Alabama Jubilee • Bye Bye Love • Duelin' Banjos • The Entertainer • Foggy Mountain Breakdown • Great Balls of Fire • Lady of Spain • Orange Blossom Special • (Ghost) Riders in the Sky • Rocky Top • San Antonio Rose • Tennessee Waltz • UFO-TOFU • You Are My Sunshine • and more.
00699565 Book/Online Audio... $27.50

HAL•LEONARD®

Prices, contents, and availability subject to change without notice.

Visit Hal Leonard online at **www.halleonard.com**
0419
270